Weapons of
Mass Deliverance

Nancy Kaplan

xulon PRESS

Table of Contents

Important Information...vii

Dedication ix

Preface: Before You Begin to Read...................................xi

Chapter 1: Unleashing Weapons of Mass Deliverance 13

Chapter 2: Go Through the Gates 19

Chapter 3: A Journey with Moses 23

Chapter 4: Wandering in the Wilderness.........................35

Chapter 5: The God-Chosen Fast 47

Chapter 6: Gates — Shadows and Symbols.....................53

Chapter 7: Where are the Gates?...................................61

Chapter 8: What Occurred at the Gates?.........................69

Chapter 9: The City of God...89

Chapter 10: Enemy at the Gate 97

Chapter 11: Gates of Prayer 119

Chapter 12: Entering Through the Narrow Gate............161

Special Note to Intercessors 167

Important Information

※◎◇※

"Behold, How good and how pleasant it is for brethren to dwell together in unity... for there the Lord commanded the blessing, even life forevermore." (Psalm 133:1-3b)

Over these last few years, it has been very exciting to see how the Spirit of God is revealing many different facets and views of the authority available to the Body of Messiah as Gatekeepers. The Spirit is speaking this truth to many different people in many different places around the globe. There are a few anointed servants in the Body of Messiah who have influenced me, and whose teaching has, in some way, had an influence on the fullness of what God was revealing to me as I wrote this book. Likewise, I know that my teaching and my ministry have also had an impact on others who are teaching and writing on this same topic.

Throughout this book, you will notice that I have mentioned the names and ministries of some of those who have influenced me and blessed me with their teaching. If this topic is of interest to you, I would suggest that you also read their books to gain even deeper understanding. Besides those mentioned through this book, I am sure that there are others who are teaching some of these same wonderful revelations as well. Perhaps Peter described it best. *"Knowing this first, that no prophecy of the scripture is a matter of ones own interpretation. For no prophecy was ever made by an act of human will, but men moved by the Holy Spirit spoke from God."* (2 Peter 1:20-21)

May God continue to use all of these ministries to teach these important truths – not because they are our own revelations – but because they contain wisdom that could only be revealed by the Holy Spirit.

My heart's prayer is that this material will reveal more of God to you — *and that it will give you deeper insight into who you are in Him.*

Dedication

This book is dedicated to my mom, Vivian, who because of her love and patience made it possible for me to complete the work I was called to do. I would also like to take this opportunity to express my heartfelt gratitude to Iris, for encouraging me to write down the vision; Dr. Lori Greenwood for her encouragement and involvement in the development of the manuscript; and Bishop Allen Coleman for his wisdom and prayer support in seeing this project to it's completion. Most of all, I would like to give glory to God through whom this book was made possible.

Before You Begin to Read...

J esus is a Jew. Think about it... Jesus was born a Jew, practiced Judaism, and became a Jewish Rabbi – a teacher of the Holy Scriptures. Somehow, over the course of history, many have come to think of Jesus as only the God of the Christian faith – *and have forgotten that He lived and died a Jew.*

Having been born a Jew, Jesus would have had a Jewish name. In fact, He would have never heard Himself called, "Jesus." The name, "Jesus," is merely man's attempt to convert His Hebrew name into the Greek language. Messiah was really called by the name "Yeshua."

In January of 1983, for the first time, someone began to show me Yeshua as Messiah through the Old Testament scriptures. As a Jew, I began to see Him for who He really was – and is – *the Jewish Savior.* I received Him as my Messiah, and became a believer.

> *"Who hath ascended up into heaven, or descended? Who hath gathered the wind in his fists? Who hath bound the waters in a*

> *garment? Who hath established all the ends of the earth? What is his name, and what is his son's name, if thou canst tell?"* (Proverbs 30:4)

God's Son is named *Yeshua.* The Jewish prophet, Micah told us that Yeshua would be born out of the city of Bethlehem. (Micah 5:2) Another Jewish prophet, named Isaiah, told us that Messiah would be born of a virgin. (Isaiah 7:14) He also recorded that Yeshua would come as a child, be given to us as a son, and yet would hold the titles: Wonderful Counselor, Mighty God, Everlasting Father, and Prince of Peace. (Isaiah 9:6) Isaiah also saw His suffering... understanding that Yeshua would be wounded for our sin, bruised for our iniquity, chastised for our peace, and have stripes laid on His back to purchase our healing. (Isaiah 53) If you are reading this, and you do not yet know Yeshua as Messiah, then I want you to take a moment to turn to Chapter 12: *Entering Through the Narrow Gate* at the very end of this book.

Throughout this book, you will notice the use of the name Yeshua Ha Mashiach (pronounced: ye-shoo-aah ha ma-shee-aah) instead, or in place of the name, Jesus Christ. In addition, you will notice the use of the word, "Messiah," like "Mashiach," it is also a Hebrew word for Christ. Both of these names, the Hebrew: Messiah and the Greek: Christ mean, "anointed," or "the anointed One."

I pray, that as you continue to read, the Ruach Ha Kodesh (the Holy Spirit) will truly reveal Yeshua Ha Mashiach to you.

CHAPTER 1

Unleashing Weapons of Mass Deliverance

※❀※

A weapon is only effective in the hand of a warrior. As the Spirit began to reveal to me the power of the material in this book, it became clear that He was showing me a very significant weapon. A weapon so significant, it had the ability to deliver masses of people trapped under the influence of sin and the forces of darkness. From that moment on, my mission was to get the weapon into the hands of the warriors. Who are these warriors that will operate as God's Weapons of Mass Deliverance? The worshipers, the musicians, and the dancers are God's WMD's.

> *"Praise the LORD! Sing to the LORD a new song, and his praise in the congregation of the godly ones.*
>
> *Let Israel be glad in his maker; Let the sons of Zion rejoice in their King.*
>
> *Let them praise his name with dancing; let them sing praises to him with timbrel and lyre.*

For the Lord takes pleasure in his people; he will beautify the afflicted ones with salvation.

Let the godly ones exult in glory: let them sing for joy on their beds.

Let the high praises of God be in their mouth, and a two-edged sword in their hand;

To execute vengeance on the nations, and punishment on the peoples;

To bind their kings with chains, and their nobles with fetters of iron;

To execute on them the judgment written; this is an honor for all his godly ones."

Praise the LORD!" (Psalm 149)

In our generation, I believe God will use the Worshipers, the Musicians, and the Dancers as agents of mass deliverance. The text (above) from Psalm 149 really makes that clear to us. It explains that those who praise His name through dance, song, and instruments are able to execute vengeance, binding kings and nobles – restraining strongholds, principalities, and powers — with chains and fetters of iron. Wow! When the Worshipers, Musicians, and Dancers unite together, they become a formidable force in entering the presence of God, piercing through the darkness in the heavenlies, and allowing the shekinah glory of God to come through to the earth. The power of these worship forces uniting can impact multitudes in cities and nations – allowing people everywhere to come to the saving knowledge of the Most High God.

All over the globe, God has been speaking to many about becoming Worship Warriors. As an intercessor, I have seen a shift in the spirit that is emphasizing dance as a form of warfare against the enemy. God is raising up Worship Warriors to declare His Word at the Gates. As the "WMD

Teams" unite with those making declarations and intercession at the Gates, they welcome the protecting presence of God. The beauty of this strategy is that the enemy can't see where these "missiles" of prayer and declarations are coming from. God's glory acts as a protective covering. Unity is the key. Unity of purpose between these three factions of worshippers, aimed at one target, will ultimately bring transformation to churches, cites, and nations. I think Psalm 140 gives the best illustration of this:

> *"I said to the LORD, Thou art my God; Give ear O LORD, to the voice of my supplications, O GOD the Lord, the strength of my salvation, Thou hast covered my head in the day of battle. Do not grant, O LORD, the desires of the wicked; Do not promote his evil device, lest they be exalted. As for the head of those who surround me, May the mischief of their lips cover them. Selah."*
> (Psalm 140:6-9)

In the midst of praise and worship, God Himself covers our heads in the day of battle.

Psalm 87:2 states, *"The Lord loves the gates of Zion more than all the dwellings of Jacob."* A gate – or a door – swings two ways. In order for us to enter into God's presence, we must go through Jesus/Yeshua to get to the Father. Yeshua is the only way to the Father (John 14:6). Once we have come into the Father's presence, He is able to move through us – like a gate – to touch the lost, the oppressed, and the dying of our generation. As the Worshipers, Musicians and Dancers praise God, He inhabits their praise – *He dwells in their praise.* As they go through Messiah into the Father, the Father goes through their praise into the world. As these worshipers use their authority at the gates, the enemy is defeated and God is exalted!

Even in the accounts of the Old Testament, we know that God used the tribe of Worshipers, Musicians and Dancers (known as Judah) to enter into battle. The Word of God is filled with evidence to sustain the understanding that He is going to use the Worshipers to move His people through the gates and to bring attack against His enemies.

> *"In the morning, O LORD, Thou wilt hear my voice; In the morning I will order my prayer to Thee and eagerly watch. For Thou art not a God who takes pleasure in wickedness; No evil dwells with Thee. The boastful shall not stand before Thine eyes; Thou dost hate all who do iniquity. Thou dost destroy those who speak falsehood; The LORD abhors the man of bloodshed and deceit. But as for me, by Thine abundant lovingkindness I will enter Thy house, At Thy holy temple I will bow in reverence for Thee."* (Psalm 5:3-7)

> *"The Lord lives, and blessed be my rock; And exalted be the God of my salvation, The God who executes vengeance for me, And subdues peoples under me. He delivers me from my enemies; Surely Thou dost lift me above those who rise up against me; thou dost rescue me from the violent man. Therefore I will give thanks to Thee among the nations, O LORD, And I will sing praises to Thy name."* (Psalm 18:46-49)

> *"He who offers a sacrifice of thanksgiving honors Me; And to him who orders his way*

aright I shall show the salvation of God."
(Psalm 50:23)

*"But as for me, I shall sing of thy strength;
Yes, I shall joyfully sing of thy lovingkindness
in the morning, For Thou hast been my
stronghold, And a refuge in the day of my
distress. O my strength, I will sing praises to
thee; For God is my stronghold, the God who
shows me lovingkindness."* (Psalm 59:16-17)

I asked the Holy Spirit to quicken this revelation to you. I pray that you see the strategy that God has for you to implement. Twelve is a very key number. It represents governmental authority. There are 12 gates in the New Jerusalem, there are twelve strongholds, twelve tribes, and 12 angels at the gates in Revelation 21:10-12. My prayer is that God would raise up groups of 12 intercessors all over the world to go through the Gates! (Isaiah 62:10-11)

As you read further into this book, we will dissect a key text of scripture from Isaiah 62. For years, I knew that Isaiah 62:10-12 had to do with intercession yet it was not until the end of 1999 that the Lord opened up the revelation of that scripture. You are a gate. You are a seat of authority. Through you, God will touch the world. It is my desire to share with you the power of what the Lord has revealed to me, but the next step is counting on you! You must take action by using material in this book and applying it to your times of intercession. I beseech each one of you to ask the Holy Spirit to teach you how He would have you go through the gates.

When God first began to show me these truths, it was at the lowest point of my life. I had been in bed an entire year and was having no victory in my life. I had been stripped of everything — *I mean everything.* All that was left was my trusty dog, Yofe and lots of tears. I felt that my life had been destroyed. Yet out of the ashes of my life, the revelation you are about to read was illuminated to me, and subsequently a ministry was born. Many of you that will be reading this book don't know me and may never meet me, but I can tell you that I have already been interceding for you — and I will continue to do so. You might ask, "Why?" The answer is simple. I know that without intercession hearts remain cold as stone, sinners are not convicted, and the kingdom of God suffers. I also know that as you pour your heart out in intercession, sometimes you feel that no one is interceding for you. I am here to tell you that God has put you on my heart. I will pray for you. So I say to you:

"Lift up your heads O ye Gates that the KING OF GLORY may come in!"

CHAPTER 2

Go Through,
Go Through the Gates

✻✦✻

*"Go through, go through the gates! Clear
the way for the people; Build up, build up the
highway; Remove the stones, lift up a stan-
dard over the peoples.*

*Behold, the LORD has proclaimed to the end
of the earth, Say to the daughter of Zion Lo,
your salvation comes; Behold His reward is
with Him, and His recompense before Him.*

*And they will call them, The holy people, The
redeemed of the LORD; and you will be
called, Sought out, A city not forsaken."*
(Isaiah 62:10-12)

Listen to what God is saying through the Prophet Isaiah.
"Go through, go through the gates…" "Go" is an imperative. Imperative means essential, necessary, crucial, critical,
important. Therefore, to God it is essential, necessary,

important, crucial, and critical to go through the gates. He even has Isaiah say it twice. "Go" is an order. "Go" is a command. "Go" is a call to action. "Go through the gates." There is more than one gate... the command is to go through the gates (plural). Clear the way for the unsaved peoples. We are commanded to clear the way for the peoples to come to the Lord.

Clear the way of the Lord in the wilderness and build up a highway for the Holy Spirit. The Holy Spirit wants a highway of holiness. The unclean will not walk there. Let's think about that for a moment. What is a highway? The basic purpose and function of a highway is to allow you to get from one place to another quickly. A highway doesn't have any detours. A highway doesn't have any traffic lights. A highway doesn't have any stop signs. Highways are constructed to eliminate delays and allow you to move — *fast!* Right? With that in mind, listen to what God is saying. "Clear the way for the Lord in the wilderness. Build up a highway, and remove the stones. Proclaim to the daughter of Zion, behold, your salvation comes (You're salvation/ Yeshua is coming!) and the reward is with Him." The reward is Yeshua! The reward is God, Himself — but we need to clear the way and open up the highway, so the world can see Him and come to Him.

When we read this text from Isaiah, we see that we are commanded to go through the gates. We're commanded to build up a highway. We're commanded to remove the stones and to clear the way for the Lord in the wilderness.

You'll notice when you read the Bible, that most scriptures have a "mate." By that I mean a verse that is similar and acts as a confirmation. You know, everything in the Bible is confirmed in the mouth of at least two witnesses (Matthew 18:16). *"But if he does not listen to you, take one or two more with you, so that BY THE MOUTH OF TWO OR THREE WITNESSES EVERY FACT MAY BE CONFIRMED."*

Having said that, let's look at this "mate" scripture in Isaiah 40:3-5.

> *"A voice is calling, Clear the way for the LORD in the wilderness; Make smooth in the desert a highway for our God. Let every valley be lifted up, And every mountain and hill be made low; And let the rough ground become a plain, And the rugged terrain a broad valley; Then the glory of the LORD will be revealed, And all flesh will see it together; For the mouth of the LORD has spoken."* (Isaiah 40:3-5)

A voice is calling, *"Clear the way for the Lord in the wilderness."* Does that sound familiar? *"Make smooth in the desert a highway for our God."* There's that highway again. *"Let every valley be lifted up And every mountain and hill be made low; And let the rough ground become a plain And the rugged terrain a broad valley"*. Now look at the next word... **Then**. *"**Then** the glory of the Lord will be revealed, And all flesh will see it together; for the mouth of the Lord has spoken."*

The glory of the Lord will come *after* we clear the way for the Lord in the wilderness. Make a highway! There are certain things that must be done through intercession before the glory of the Lord is revealed. Isaiah gives us keys to what those things are. One key, found in Isaiah 62:10, has to do with "stones." We must remove the stones. What do stones represent in the Bible? Stones represent hard hearts – or hard places in our hearts.

> *"Moreover I will give you a new heart and put a new spirit within you. I will remove the heart of stone from your flesh and give you a*

heart of flesh." (Ezekiel 36:26)

A stone represents a heart. God is saying, "I'll take out your heart of stone and I'll put in a heart of flesh. I'll put My Spirit within you. I'll cause you to walk in My ways and be obedient to My commandments." When you have a heart of stone, you don't walk in His commandments... do you? God is saying, "Remove the stones." Our faith is much more than having a salvation encounter with Yeshua; it's fellow-shipping with Him, and allowing Him to take us through the process of sanctification. We can have stones in our own heart, even though we've had a "heart transplant" through the experience of salvation. We all have those little hard places in our heart — stones. God wants to remove those stones from our hearts.

To make this point even clearer, let's take a journey in the wilderness...

CHAPTER 3

A Journey with Moses

༄༅

"Now the LORD said to Moses, Come up to
Me on the mountain and remain there, and I
will give you the stone tablets with the law
and the commandment which I have written
for their instruction." (Exodus 24:12)

Has God ever said to you, "Come up on the mountain and remain there?" How many times in prayer have we gotten through the gates, and gotten into God's presence, and then we don't really know what to do next? We're just there. Do we wait on God? We get there, but when He wants to share secrets of Himself, we just sort of walk away. We just about get into His presence and we don't have the patience to wait. We don't know what to do... so we leave. Realize that when God called Moses up to the mountain, He called him up there for 40 days! I'm not suggesting that we leave our homes and go up to spend time on the mountain for 40 days, but what about 40 minutes? Can we wait and linger in His presence for 40 minutes? Can we linger for just a little while?

He said to Moses, "Come up to the mountain and remain there." What did God do as a result of that time? God said, "I will give you stone tablets with the law and the commandments which I have written for the people's instructions." What did God give him? Stone tablets. What do stones represent? **Hearts**. *God gave Moses His heart.*

What is the law or instruction? It is Yeshua Ha Mashiach – Jesus Christ — the Cornerstone. Remember Yeshua came to fulfill the law. When God gave those two tablets to Moses, He gave him His heart. It was a glimpse into the future – a picture of Yeshua.

> *"Then Moses turned and went down from the mountain with the two tablets of the testimony in his hand, tablets which were written on both sides; they were written on one side and the other."* (Exodus 32:15)

Moses left the presence of God to return down the mountain and give the people God's heart. It took him 40 days, but God had given him His heart, which was the law — or His teaching and instruction. Basically, it was God's way of saying, "Follow My teachings and instructions and you will be blessed, disregard My teachings and instructions and you will be cursed." Moses wanted to give the people the law and the instruction, so he began the journey down the mountain to give the people God's heart. Let's take a look at what happened after that...

> *"And it came about, as soon as Moses came near the camp, that he saw the calf and the dancing; and Moses' anger burned and he threw the tablets from his hands and shattered them at the foot of the mountain."* (Exodus 32:19)

Moses threw the tablets down, but more than the tablets got broken. It was a picture of God's heart being shattered. He literally broke God's heart. It broke God's heart to see the people moving into idolatry. God had just taken them out of Egypt. He had revealed Himself through signs and wonders. He had parted the Red Sea. He had taken them out of slavery. Then, when He wants to give them His heart, His law and instruction, they break it! Now what is God going to do? His heart and His law or instruction have been broken.

> *"Now the LORD said to Moses," Cut out for yourself two stone tablets like the former ones, and I will write on the tablets the words that were on the former tablets which you shattered."* (Exodus 34:1)

The first time that Moses was on the mountain with God, God had already prepared the stone tablets and gave them to Moses; but now, God says, "Moses, *you* cut out two stone tablets for yourself."

Have you ever climbed a mountain? The air in higher altitudes is a lot lighter. It's harder to breathe. You get tired. Now, not only does Moses have to take himself up the mountain again, but he also has to cut 2 stone tablets. Do you know what that is giving us a picture of? It's a picture of intercession.

When you intercede for people, you are the one who has to take the hearts of men to God. You're standing in the gap between God and man. You're taking those hearts up the mountain to God asking Him to write His law or teachings and instructions upon their hearts. It's work! You pay a price in intercession. You follow in the same footsteps as Moses.

> *"Behold, days are coming, declares the LORD, when I will make a new covenant*

with the house of Israel and the house of Judah; not like the covenant which I made with their fathers in the day I took them by the hand to bring them out of the land of Egypt. My covenant which they broke, although I was a husband to them, declares the Lord." (Jeremiah 31:31-32)

God was a husband to the Israelites when He took them out of the bondage of Egypt. He led them with a fire at night and with a cloud by day. He kept them warm. He fed them. He took care of them. He protected them. He spared them from the Egyptians who were coming after them. He parted the Red Sea for them. He was a husband to them. He loved them, but they still broke His covenant. Do we ever break His covenants?

"But this is the covenant which I will make with the house of Israel after those days, declares the LORD, I'll put my law within them, and on their heart I will write it; and I will be their God, and they shall be My people.

And they shall not teach again, each man his neighbor and each man his brother, saying, 'Know the LORD,' for they shall all know Me, from the least of them to the greatest of them, declares the LORD, for I will forgive their iniquity, and their sin I will remember no more." (Jeremiah 31:33-34)

At first, God put the law on the stone tablets and gave it to Moses. Now God is saying, "I'm going to put my law *within* them and write it on their hearts." God is no longer going to write on the stone tablets. He's going to write on human hearts. I will be their God. They will be my people. I'll put Yeshua and my Spirit in them. Each man and his brother will know Me. God's desire is to write His law or teachings and instruction upon our hearts.

What happens to us in intercession? When we start praying for others, we've got to make sure that the very things we're praying about for somebody else to be delivered from are not operating in us. Think about that for a moment. How can we pray something out of somebody else if it is in operation in us? God says that He is faithful and just to forgive us if we confess our sins.

> *"If we confess our sins, He is faithful and righteous to forgive us our sins and to cleanse us from all unrighteousness."* (1 John 1:9)

We cannot change ourselves. We can't change our own heart. Only God can change our heart. The first step requires us to acknowledge our sin. You know, we can sit there and say, "Oh God, that person has so much pride. I just wish that You would deal with their pride." Maybe God wants to deal with your pride? First, we need to earnestly say to God, "Change my heart. Create in me a clean heart. Renew a steadfast spirit within me. Don't cast me away from Your Holy Spirit. **Then** I'll teach transgressors Your ways and sinners shall be converted." Hallelujah! Are you with me?

Let me talk about "stones" on a more personal level. As believers, the Lord has given us a heart transplant. He's taken out that heart of stone and He's put in a heart of flesh; however, as we go through life, things happen to us. The heart that He has given to us becomes a little hardened in spots. When we first got saved, we were on that glory ride, and the grass looked so much greener. Remember? We were in love with God and in love with everybody. Then six months passed, and God really began to show us the state of our heart. We start feeling a little bit resentful towards certain things that happened to us. We may feel a little anger or unforgiveness. Situations happen and we may feel like we have a "right" to our emotions. We may have made "religious statements" like, "I choose to forgive them, God." If you confess your sins and repent, He deals with your stones.

Let me give you an illustration to help clarify this point. I was at a friend's house and I saw that she had a fish made out of glass. We are like that fish. Usually, we have big mouths like fish! God tries to tame our tongue. A fish, or the symbol of the fish, represents a Christian — and yet, some fish have many stones inside. When God first fills us with His Spirit, He doesn't have a whole lot of room to operate because we have all sorts of stones in the way. So, God starts talking to us about removing the bitterness, judgment, resentment, and the critical spirit from our lives. In addition, there might be some smaller stones inside us that are a little harder to get out, like emotional wounds or disappointing things that happened to us over the course of our life. Ultimately, God wants us to just flow with Him. Now, imagine that glass fish that I mentioned just a moment ago. If I put that fish loaded down with stones into the water, you know that it will sink! Get a picture of that in your mind. That fish is not going to move with the Spirit; it's not able to, because it's too weighted down. God wants to remove those stones! He's not going to remove them all at once. We wouldn't know what to do if He did that. He's going to take His time and reveal and unveil each stone. As you fast and pray, He loosens the bonds of wickedness in your life. He undoes the bands of the yoke. He lets the oppressed go free. He breaks every yoke while you fast and wait on Him.

Isaiah 58:6 says: *"Is this not the fast which I choose, To loosen the bonds of wickedness, To undo the bands of the yoke, And to let the oppressed go free, And break every yoke?"*

As a result, you'll have more of a chance to swim a little bit. You will find that you have more freedom to move. I'd like to share a story about something that happened to me when I lived in Israel. I lived in Israel for exactly forty months. Forty is the number of testing and trials. I spent 2 years in Jerusalem in my own apartment, but the Lord was moving me to an area north of Tel Aviv. Before He moved me there, I went to the home of a friend who needed my help for a few weeks. I left my apartment. I left all my furnishings and my appliances with my roommate there, because she needed them. I put my personal things in storage, except for my prized piano, which I loved. I had given it to the friend I was going to help for a couple of weeks. I already knew that God had confirmed to me that He had opened up a place for me north of Tel Aviv. For two weeks before I left Jerusalem, I told this friend that I would come and help her while she recovered from surgery. Near the end of those two weeks, I was schlepping. Do you know what "schlepping" means? It is a Jewish word that means *to carry or to lug something*. I didn't have a car. I either walked or rode the bus. I knew she liked watermelon. It happened to be in the summer, and watermelon was available. I would take a walk and schlep watermelons home for her. So, there I was walking in very hot weather, to schlep these watermelons for her in addition to everything involved in taking care of her while she was recovering. Well, just a few days before it was time for me to go, we got into a conflict. I was doing my best to clean her house, and cook for her, and take care of her, but evidently she didn't like the way I was doing it. One day, she looked straight at me and she insulted me. She used vulgar language and really said some horrible things! I thought to myself, "How demeaning! How degrading!" Can you imagine yourself in my position? Here I was trying to help her and she insulted me! I'll tell you, I think I added a few stones that day. I was angry and resentful. I was so upset that I took my dog and walked the 5 miles back to my old apartment that I'd just left 2 weeks before. My roommate had my $1000.00 leather couch and my $800.00 dining room set and all of my appliances. She still had 2 empty bedrooms. I explained to her what had happened. I said," I can't go back there." Much to my shock she responded, "Well, you can't stay here!" *Hold on a minute*...she's using all of my appliances and furniture, and she says I can't stay there!! I asked her, "Why?" She said she already had another roommate and they agreed that they wouldn't do anything unless they talked to each other first. The new roommate wasn't there and she didn't know how to get hold of her. I thought, "If I have to take one of my mattresses and bring it down these 54 stairs and sleep in the park downstairs on the outside of this building I'll do it — but I'm *not* going back to that house!!!!!" So now, things are getting worse. More stones are being added. It was awful!!!! It was really bad. I was angry and bitter. I had no idea what to do. I started walking back and I thought, "I have no place to go." I can't afford to go to a hotel. I ended up going over to some people's apartment that I hadn't yet said good-bye to. By the time I got there, my roommate called me and apologized. She told me to stay at the apartment, which I did for those last few days before I left for Tel Aviv. By the way the other friend also apologized at a later date. Do you know that all of that happened in just a few hours of time?

The reason I told you that story is to show you that sometimes God puts us in certain situations to reveal what is *really* in our hearts. In the end, I had to forgive. At times, we're all capable of this kind of behavior. Sometimes, we're on the other side of the situation. We're the roommates that say, "No... you can't stay here." Sometimes we can be like the woman who used vulgar and insulting language. I'm sure many of you could identify with all the sides and personalities in that story. Through these types of situations, God reveals what's in our own hearts. He wants to clean us up so we can flow with Him. He really wants to blast those stones out of our life completely!

Stones in Antimony

> *"Oh, afflicted one, storm-tossed and not comforted. Behold I will set your stones in antimony."* (Isaiah 54:11)

What's antimony? What does God mean when He says He'll set your stones in antimony? In some Bibles it says fair colors and your foundations.

> *"And your foundations I will lay in sapphires. Moreover, I will make your battle-ments of rubies, And your gates of crystal, And your entire wall of precious stones"* (Isaiah 54:12)

God's going to set our stones in antimony... What does that mean? You know there are certain stones in our lives; whether it's bitterness, anger, resentment, judgmental attitudes, old wounds or whatever they may be, that we confess and bring before God. But, even after we confess, somehow we do not come down completely to the root of the problem. The surface situation is taken care of, but the root problem is still there. God wants to exterminate the root. The reason He wants to exterminate the root of the problem is because He knows without that the fruit will be rotten. When He says He's going to set your stones in antimony, it means He's going to blast those things right out of your life!

I looked up the definition of antimony because I didn't

have a clue what it was. Antimony is a trivalent or a pentavalent metalloid element that is commonly found in most forms of explosives. Well, that got me excited! Penta means *five*. Tri means *three*. Valent means *having or adding a degree of power to a radical or an element.* In other words, you're going to add the power of 3 to an element. The power of the Father, Son and the Holy Spirit are going to be added to you to blast those things out of your life. They have the power to go to the radical, to go to the element, to go to the deepest part and blast it out of your life. The other term is Pentavalent. What is penta? Penta means "five." It's referring to the five-fold ministry: the apostles, prophets, evangelists, teachers, and pastors. God's going to use His five fold ministry gifts to take out some stones! He's going to use those instruments of His to blast those stones out of your life. Why does God want to blast those stones out of your lives? So the Holy Spirit can flow freely, enabling you to build up that highway that God can move through. God will take that wilderness that's in you and remove it, so that His presence and His glory can come through you. Then the glory of the Lord will come. When we're emptied out, then the glory of the Lord will come and all flesh will see it. The mouth of the Lord has spoken it. When we pray, we can remind God of His Word. He's given us this promise. "God, You said You would set my stones in antimony!

Let's look at the next verse, Isaiah 54:12. What does it mean to lay your foundations in sapphires? Sapphires are gemstones of a blue color. Blue represents the anointing. Our foundation is going to be in the anointing. Our foundation is going to be in the presence of God! Old things have passed away and new things have come!

What does it mean to have battlements of rubies? Where are we going to battle from? Are we going to battle from a ruby? A ruby has a deep red color. We're going to battle from the position of the blood of Messiah, which cleanses us of all iniquity. Hallelujah!

What about the crystal or carbuncle as some translations call it? Your gates will be of crystal. The enemies attack at the gates. Your gates are transparent. Crystal is transparent. You'll be able to see the enemy. You'll know who the enemy is. We don't wrestle against flesh and blood but against principalities and powers.

> *"For our struggle is not against flesh and blood, but against the rulers, against the powers, against the world forces of this darkness, against the spiritual forces of wickedness in the heavenly places."* (Ephesians 6:12)

You will see the enemy when he's coming. You won't look at the person. You'll look beyond the person. It may take some work to separate the person from the real enemy in the spirit — but God can get us there! Your gates will be of crystal and your entire wall will be of precious stone. As God does this work in us, His glory will be revealed – and everyone will see it!

> *"Let every valley be lifted up, And every mountain and hill be made low; And let the rough ground become a plain, And the rugged terrain a broad valley; Then the glory of the LORD will be revealed, And all flesh will see it together; For the mouth of the LORD has spoken."* (Isaiah 40:4-5)

There are certain things that grieve the Holy Spirit, and there are certain things that draw Him. Speaking about the blood, singing about the blood, and having that understanding of the blood draws the Holy Spirit. Exalting Yeshua draws the Holy Spirit. Simply acknowledging the Holy

Spirit draws Him. But if we decide to pick up some stones in our life, we put Him at a distance. He's not distancing Himself permanently; He's just waiting until we repent so that He can be in fellowship with us. He never leaves us; we leave Him. Create in me a clean heart Lord and renew a steadfast spirit within me. Cast me not away from Your presence. Don't take Your Holy Spirit away from me. **Then,** I'll teach transgressors Your ways, and sinners shall be converted to You. Hallelujah!!

> *"Create in me a clean heart, O God, And renew a steadfast spirit within me. Do not cast me away from Thy presence, And do not take Thy Holy Spirit from me. Restore to me the joy of Thy salvation, And sustain me with a willing spirit. Then I will teach transgressors thy ways, And sinners will be converted to Thee."* (Psalm 51:10-13)

Let's take a moment just to thank God. Father, we just thank You for this teaching. We pray that every stone would be removed out of our own hearts for Your Glory. We ask that You fill Your Temple with Your Presence, God. We welcome You Holy Spirit. We ask You, LORD God, to take out of us all those things that are not pleasing to You. Reveal them to us. Cleanse Your temple. Purify Your temple, Father God. We offer You all the praise, all the glory, and all the honor. You are worthy of all praise. Thank you God that we can't do this in our own strength. We can only do all these things through You who strengthens us. We glorify You and bless You Lord. We magnify Your Holy Name. Make us that highway of Holiness, In Yeshua's Name, Amen.

CHAPTER 4

Wandering in the Wilderness

❦

Has anybody ever experienced the wilderness? Fun …isn't it? Isn't it wonderful being in the wilderness? No, it isn't fun! It's all dry – desert. God does not bring you into the wilderness so that you can have fun, but He does have a purpose for you through those wilderness experiences.

The Lord did a lot of training with me in the wilderness. Let me share something that happened to me. The Lord told me to get my citizenship in Israel, and I did. I lived there for a few years. He took me through a lot of experiences while I was living there. It was all preparation for ministry — which I didn't realize at the time. When the time there was over, I came back to the USA and landed in Washington DC. I had $300.00 in my pocket and one small suitcase. What I hadn't realized is that, while I was in Israel, my teaching certificate had expired, making me unemployable in my professional field. I didn't know what I was going to do with my life. As I was sitting there I said, "Lord, I believe You've led me on a path of destruction." Do you know what He said? "I have." He said, "I have led you on this path."

God's a good God... right? I thought He would only do good things in your life. Why would God lead you down a path of destruction? I started to say, "I've always tithed. I've always been a giver. I'm Your child. I've been obedient. You know, if I'm obedient, I'll eat the good of the land. OK God... I believe you've led me on this path of destruction. But why?" He told me to turn to Deuteronomy 8 and my eye fell on vs.15.

> *"He led you through the great and terrible wilderness, with its fiery serpents and scorpions and thirsty ground where there was no water; He brought water for you out of the rock of flint. "In the wilderness, He fed you manna, that your fathers did not know, that He might humble you, and that He might test you to do good for you in the end. Otherwise you may say in your heart, My power and the strength of my hand made me this wealth. But you shall remember the LORD your God, for it is He who is giving you the power to make wealth, that He may confirm His covenant which He swore to your fathers as it is this day."* (Deuteronomy 8:15-18)

Why does God bring you into the wilderness? He does it to humble you... to test you. Why? That He may do good for you in the end. Does it look like good is going to come out of your time in the wilderness? No, it usually doesn't look very good. Do you always pass the test in the wilderness? No. Does God give you another chance? Yes. Ultimately, His design is to do good to you in the end – no matter what it looks like when you're in the middle of it!

What are the lessons learned in the wilderness?

Lesson One: Humility. Humility is learning that God is God and we're not!

Lesson Two: Character Development. It's amazing how God changes your nature and your character in the wilderness. You almost can't believe some of the things that are going on! While you're busy asking God, "How could you allow this to happen to me?" He's allowing the time in the wilderness to build character into you.

Lesson Three: Perseverance. You learn perseverance in the wilderness. I remember for many days saying," God, please, encourage me today... please, just encourage me today, just today, please, encourage me." Nothing. The next day, "God, please, just encourage me today." Nothing. "God, please, encourage me today." Nothing. Eventually, I developed the kind of perseverance where I could encourage myself. I have a choice. I can add a few more stones inside myself and get upset with God, or I can just humble myself, encourage myself in the Lord and keep moving. But before perseverance came, I wasn't there yet. I would separate myself from God. I would argue with God. "I've been obedient. I've done everything you said to do. Now look what you've done to me." What was I doing? I was accusing God. That was pride. So there are lessons in perseverance. When you learn to move through trials and just continue on, you realize most of the time it was God carrying you and enabling you to get through those trials.

Lesson Four: Trust. You know you can't trust yourself. And you can't trust in men because we all mess things up from time-to-time. We all let each other down. You must learn to trust in God and learn to say, "God, even though you slay me, yet will I praise you."

Lesson Five: Patience. Don't we all love patience? I wish I could say that we all love to learn patience. Patience is what we need when we're learning to depend upon God. You know you have to be very careful about what you pray for because God's going to take you at your word. If we say, "God, I want to walk by faith." He says "O.K."

Let me give you an illustration of a patience lesson that I went through. I was teaching for a number of years and I went into burnout. I said, "God I need a major change in my life. I need a major change!" His idea of a major change was different than mine. My idea of a major change was... I'd like to be married, move to a nicer house, have a couple of kids, maybe get a new car. You know... a major change. God's idea of a major change was to take me out of the United States and put me into His country – Israel. I was literate in this country; illiterate in Israel. I had a car in this country; I had to walk in Israel. I had a job in this country; I had to depend on God in Israel. When I told God I wanted a major change, it was somewhat like when the children of Israel were in the desert and they said, "We want quail!" God said, "You want quail? I'll give you quail!" Then they had so much quail it was coming out of their noses.

God's thoughts are higher than our thoughts and His ways are higher than our ways. In the wilderness you learn to be grateful for the little things. We take so many things for granted. But you really learn to be grateful when you're in the wilderness. You learn thanksgiving.

Lesson Six: Gratefulness. Do you know how to stay in the wilderness? Be ungrateful. If you want to stay in the wilderness you just do these 3 things, and you can remain in the wilderness.

1. Complain
2. Murmur
3. Grumble

If you can complain, murmur and grumble, (which I used to get an A+ in) then you can remain in the wilderness, but if you learn to praise Him, give Him thanks and trust Him, you'll probably leave the wilderness a lot sooner!

God will allow a need in your life so that you may fellowship with Him at the point of that need, and experience Him in the provision. Think about a need in your life. As you begin to pray, you begin to fellowship with Him regarding that need. Think about how He has provided for you in times past. You can see His faithfulness – even out in the wilderness as you are going around that mountain! You can see where He has provided. Sometimes we're tempted to say, "How is He ever going to get me out of this?" But God will provide. He is faithful to answer our cry. We are completely assured that He will come through for us because we learned that lesson in the wilderness. When God takes you through something that can be very difficult and very trying, it's only because He wants to bless you in the end.

Lesson Seven: Dependence. Now, I want to go back to the illustration I was giving you about when I first came back to the US with $300.00 in my pocket, because really, there were a few lessons going on simultaneously – gratefulness and dependence on God. At that time, I was thinking, "Now what, Lord?" Now what are we going to do. I found out that every possession that I had stored away before I moved had been given away. Given away! Have you ever been stripped of everything? When God strips you, it's only cause He wants to add to you — but it doesn't look like that when you're right in the middle of it. What do you think I did? Well, I didn't shout, "Hallelujah!" I should have; but I didn't. I got upset! If you heard that everything that you owned had been given away what would you do? All I could do was sit around and cry. "My life is totally destroyed!" When your life is destroyed, it's because God is going to build you a new life — only it's not going to be your life. God has purchased you and made you His very own. From that day, God began to add to me.

God wants to empty the world out of us. He took the children of Israel out of Egypt, but then He had to get Egypt out of them. It was the only way to bring them into the Promised Land. God wants to bring us into the Promised Land, but He has to get some things out of us first.

Often, we think that our value is in direct proportion to the job we have, how much money we make, what kind of car we drive, and what kind of home we live in. Once every thing has been removed from you then you have to re-evaluate all of that. If everything is stripped away from you, does that mean that you're a worthless person? If you have no possessions, do you have no worth? No. You're valuable. It really has nothing to do with status. You're valuable because God has chosen you.

When I realized I was starting over with absolutely nothing, I thought, "What am I going to do to earn a living in the States?" God answered. "You're going to use your ability to speak Hebrew as your job." I had to make an adjustment here. I was used to being able to trust in my own ability. I had worked as a teacher and as a speech pathologist. I have a Master's Degree in speech and language pathology. I was used to making a good salary. As I learned the wilderness lesson of trusting God, I started a job teaching Hebrew at a synagogue, making $100 a week. No car. No possessions. No teaching credentials. No big salary… *just God.*

For the first six months I had no car. Then somebody loaned me a car. Then somebody gave me a car. It was pretty beat up (actually it was one of those cars you're embarrassed to ride in). Humility. I'm driving in this car and other people are looking out their window at me… Humility!!! But, I became grateful because it was good just to have a car. Then somebody gave me a nicer car. I was so grateful! Every single day when I got in that car I would say, "Thank you God!" Do you see how God worked gratefulness into my life? All those years, from the age of eighteen all the way into my forties, I never got in my car and thanked God. I took it for granted. Everybody has a car. I'm supposed to have a car. I'm entitled to it! God was letting me know that not everybody does have a car. I learned thanksgiving by not having a car. Well, it didn't stop there. While God was teaching me, I was learning; and because I was learning He was blessing me even more. It got to the place where I had a vision and I could see myself driving in a van. I could only see myself driving a van. Even when I didn't understand how that would happen, I was already thanking God for the van. I knew He was going to do it. Then, one day, someone sowed a seed into the ministry of $19,411.87 and today the ministry has the van — *and I drive it.* That seed paid for the van, but God wanted to teach me thanksgiving and gratefulness and dependence upon Him.

When I first got saved, I told God that I wanted to be a blessing and that I wanted His power to be demonstrated through my life. What I really didn't understand when I first told Him that, was that in order for His power to be demonstrated through my life a few lessons had to be learned. I had to decrease so He would increase. If we want God's strength to be demonstrated through our life, we've got to be weak so that He can prove himself strong on our behalf.

Whatever trial you're experiencing; whatever you're going through, know that you will experience Him in the provision. When I look back, even when I was making money in my career, I didn't even have a nickel to my name. I was making $40 thousand dollars a year and never had any money. Did I tithe? Yes, I tithed. Was it because I didn't give? No, I was a giver. It was because God determined that He needed to do some things in my life. Once He did those things good can come to me in the end.

Lessons Eight: Thanksgiving. Enter His gates with thanksgiving and His courts with praise. The sacrifice of praise honors Him. There are times we have to give Him a sacrifice of praise to enter His gates and access His presence. It's a sacrifice at times. You may be going through disillusionment? You may be going through disappointment? You may be going through anger at God? As He refines us in the wilderness, our lives give glory to God. It may not look good going into the wilderness, but as God brings you through and brings you out you will find that you are thankful for everything He added to you. Some of those rough lessons come on the road to the greatest blessings that God wants to bestow on us.

> *"Go through, go through the gates and clear the way for the peoples! Build up, build up a highway! Remove the stones! Say to the daughter of Zion, Lo your salvation comes!"*
> (Isaiah 62:10-11)

To get into His Presence, we have to have a clean heart. In order not to grieve the Holy Spirit, we need to examine the things that are in us. We need to confess and come clean. God is a Holy God. He says, "Come out from among them, be thou Holy, for I am Holy." God wants relationship and fellowship with us. He truly does love us.

Let me just give you some practical advice. In the wilderness, continue to live in the Word. Continue to sing praise and worship songs. You're not going to feel like it, but let your will and your emotions be controlled by the

Spirit. One of the best things I believe that you can do in the wilderness is just keep reading the Word. If you don't want to read it, get it on tape. Listen to it. Let it feed your spirit. Pray in tongues. Pray in the spirit. If you can do these things, you won't spend all that long out there in the wilderness. Be sensitive to what God is asking you to do. If it's uncomfortable – stick with it. Hang in there!

During the time that I was in Israel, I had two wonderful years in Jerusalem. Then, as I told you, God moved me north of Tel Aviv. He put me in the home of a couple who were somewhat controlling. Sometimes, God puts you in these situations to make you transparent. Why did He put me in the home of somebody that was controlling? Well, usually, whatever you see in somebody else is an indicator of something that is in you. So, God was dealing with me about control. God put me in that home for a number of months until I couldn't take it anymore. So I left that home. Guess what God did? He put me right back in the same situation with somebody else. I had to start the whole lesson over again. I can almost guarantee that is exactly what He will do with you too, if by your will you wiggle out of the situation He has placed you in to deal with your issues. The best thing you can do is yield to Him in the wilderness because you don't want to make any more laps around the mountain. If God's dealing with you on something, let Him do it. Get on the operating table. Hang in there, it will be over in time, and He will pull you free of it.

Hills and Valleys

Are you ready to leave the wilderness now? If so, then you need to know how to make every mountain and hill low and every valley lifted up? You're looking for level ground here. God doesn't want your emotions like a roller coaster. God doesn't want you up and down. He wants you to be stable. You know regardless of your circumstances, He wants you to trust Him, to know Him and to walk uprightly before Him.

> *"Let every valley be lifted up, and every mountain and hill be made low; and let the rough ground become a plain, and the rugged terrain a broad valley."* (Isaiah 40:4)

Mountains and hills in the Bible represent governments or governmental bodies. In this case they represent principalities or evil powers. They can be "high places" in our hearts. You know, God says to bring every thought captive to the obedience of Messiah. So there can be idols in our lives. God wants to bring those high places down.

> *"For though we walk in the flesh, we do not war according to the flesh, for the weapons of our warfare are not of the flesh, but divinely powerful for the destruction of fortresses. We are destroying speculations and every lofty thing raised up against the knowledge of God, and we are taking every thought captive to the obedience of Messiah."* (2 Corinthians 10:3-5)

Keep in mind that we're not dealing with a person — we're dealing with a spirit that may be influencing a person. So how do we do that? We do that through effective intercession. You know Yeshua is sitting at the right hand of the Father and what is He doing? He's interceding for us. He's experienced our infirmities. He knows what it's like to walk on this earth. He wants to deal with issues in our lives and break the bondages in our lives so that we can go free and have the compassion to pray for others, and see them set free. That's what effectual intercession is really about. Identifying with someone's pain or infirmity and then praying on their behalf. We need to understand all of this to go through the gates.

CHAPTER 5

The God-Chosen Fast

A s God began to develop me in prayer and intercession, I found that there were times and seasons where fasting played a critical role. There is something about fasting that moves us to a deeper place of intimacy and communion with God. If you have a desire to develop yourself in this area, I would recommend reading a book called, *A Walk in the Wilderness* by Dr. Lori Greenwood, published by Xulon Press. As the Lord began to show me the revelation of the gates, I saw fasting as an important factor – particularly at the Gate of Simeon (which we will cover in more detail in a later chapter). Let's take a look at Isaiah's teaching on fasting found in the 58th chapter.

> *"Is this not the fast which I choose, to loosen the bonds of wickedness, To undo the bands of the yoke, And to let the oppressed go free, And break every yoke?*
>
> *Is it not to divide your bread with the hungry, And bring the homeless poor into the house;*

When you see the naked, to cover him; And not to hide yourself from your own flesh?

Then your light will break out like the dawn, And your recovery will speedily spring forth; And your righteousness will go before you; And the glory of the LORD will be your rear guard.

Then you will call, and the LORD will answer; You will cry, and He will say, Here I am. If you remove the yoke from your midst, the pointing of the finger, and speaking wickedness,

And if you give yourself to the hungry, and satisfy the desire of the afflicted, Then your light will rise in darkness, And your gloom will become like midday.

And the LORD will continually guide you, And satisfy your desire in scorched places, And give strength to your bones; And you will be like a watered garden, And like a spring of water whose waters do not fail.

And those from among you will rebuild the ancient ruins; You will raise up the age-old foundations; And you will be called the repairer of the breach, the restorer of the streets in which to dwell." (Isaiah 58:6-12)

The fast that God chooses is to loosen the bonds of wickedness to undo the bands of the yoke... To let the oppressed go free and to break every yoke. Didn't Yeshua say, "Come to me all who are weary and heavy-laden and I will give you rest?" He also said "Learn of me, come to me and I will give you rest." He said, "My yoke is easy and My burden is light." (Matthew 11:28-30) What is His yoke? Remember when Yeshua said, "The spirit of the Lord is upon me for he has anointed me to set the captives free and mend the broken-hearted. To set at liberty those who are bruised?" (Luke 4:18) That is the fast that God chooses! A fast that will loose the bonds of wickedness, that will undo the yokes, and let the oppressed go free.

"Is it not to divide your bread with the hungry?" What are you doing when you're dividing your bread with the hungry? What does it mean? How do you divide your bread with the hungry? You share the Bread of Life. Think about Yeshua. He was born in Bethlehem. In Hebrew, Bethlehem is pronounced Beit Lechem, which literally means, *house of bread.* Isn't that interesting? He came out of the House of Bread and gave Himself to us.

In Judaism there are 2 prayers that are prayed every Friday night when the Jewish community observe what Christians would call "communion." Interestingly enough many Christians are beginning to embrace the Jewish roots of their faith and observe the Sabbath as it is given to us to celebrate. Jews and many Christians alike have bread & wine and pray a blessing over the bread and wine and then divide the bread and give a little piece to everyone. The blessing that Jewish people recite every Sabbath is: Blessed art thou, O LORD our God, King of the universe who brings forth the bread from the earth. Isn't that awesome. The Jewish people are remembering Him. Every time you say this prayer you're remembering the One Who brings forth the bread from the earth. God is saying that this is the fast that He has chosen. *"Is it not to divide your bread with the hungry and to bring the homeless poor into the house?"* It's not just giving up food, but sharing Yeshua with others.

Are we talking about people without a house? What's He talking about here? Bring them to His House. It doesn't matter if they have a million dollars, God looks at them and says, "You're poor." Bring the homeless poor into the house...into His House. Have you ever thought about it this way?

"And when you see the naked to cover him." What does that mean? Do you see any naked people outside of your own house? If you see a naked person then cover them, but that is not everything the verse is explaining to us. It means don't expose your brother's sin. If somebody has fallen in a transgression or a sin, don't expose him or her. Don't make them naked in front of others — cover them. Love covers a multitude of sins.

"When you see the naked to cover him and not hide yourself from your own flesh." Boy, we can be nice with each other, but sometimes when we're with our families we can be very different. There was a time when the LORD convicted me in this area. I was guilty. I was not the person I should have been with my mom. So, I acted one way with others, and then was hard on my mom. So, God started dealing with me. "Be who you are all the time, Nancy. You know you're a new creature in Messiah and old things are passed away and all things are new. Why are you acting the old way with your mom? Why is she able to push those buttons?" The point I'm trying to make is that God wants to clean us up! That's the fast He chooses for us. It's not always about exterior actions – it's about change on the inside.

The fast, which God chooses, is to loosen the bonds of wickedness, to undo the bands of the yoke, to let the oppressed go free and to break every yoke. Is it not to divide your bread with the hungry? Remember what that means now? I'm repeating it because I want you to get it. When you bring someone who is spiritually homeless into church you are entering into the fast that God chooses. When you don't uncover the sin of your sister, that's the fast that God chooses. Now what happens if you enter into that fast? *"Then your light will break forth like the dawn. And your recovery will speedily spring forth."* Have you ever been in the darkness? It is dark no matter which way you go and which direction you go. God says that if you enter into His fast that your light will break forth like the dawn and your recovery will speedily spring forth. Hallelujah! Anybody sick? Enter in! I mean enter into the fast that God chooses. Your righteousness will go before you, and the glory of the Lord will be your rear guard. Righteousness goes before you and makes a way for you. God makes a way for you. God makes a way where there seems to be no way. He makes a way, where your righteousness will go before you. Do we want our righteousness to go before us? Do we want the glory to be our rear guard? We want that so we need to enter into that fast.

"Then you will call and the Lord will answer. You will cry and He will say, Here I am, if you remove the yoke from your midst, the pointing of the finger and the speaking wickedness." That's a big IF! *If* you remove the yoke out of your midst, the pointing of the finger—accusations judgments, gossip, false reports and the speaking of wickedness. If you begin to change in this area, then God will answer you. It's a conditional term. If you do your part, He does His part.

"If you give yourself to the hungry and satisfy the desire of the afflicted then your light will rise in darkness and your gloom will become like midday." Listen to that promise. The Lord will continually guide you and satisfy your desire in scorched places and you will be like a well-watered garden, like a spring of water whose waters do not fail. Think about a spring of water whose water does not fail. A spring of water brings forth life. God's promise is that YOU will bring forth life!

"And those from among you will rebuild the ancient

ruins and you will raise up the age old foundations and you will be called the repairer of the breach, the restorer of the streets to dwell."

We've got some things to think about in here. God gives us some promises of what He will do if we take the yoke out of our midst, the pointing of the finger and the speaking of wickedness. See there's some conditions to His promises, but that is the fast that God chooses.

So many times when we think of a fast, we think of giving up something — and that is true, we're giving up something. Did you ever think about a fast of words? Did you ever think about a fast of bringing a spiritually homeless person into God's house? When you see the naked to cover him? Have you ever thought about that as entering into a fast? He says in His Word that if we abide in Him and His Word abides in us, that we'll know the truth and the truth will set us free. He wants to reveal that truth to us. He wants to reveal truth to us, and set us free.

CHAPTER 6

Gates —
Shadows and Symbols

A gate is a seat of authority. How do we know that a gate is a seat of authority? Yeshua said in John 14:6: *"I am the way, the truth, and the life, no one comes to the Father but through me."* We must go through Yeshua in order to get to the Father. So what does that make Yeshua? He's a gate. Yeshua is the only gate to the Father.

In John 10:9, it says, *"I am the door; if anyone enters through me, he shall be saved, and go in and out, and find pasture."* Again, we see Yeshua as being a gate.

In Matthew 16:18, Yeshua is talking to Peter. *"And I also say to you that you are Peter, and upon this rock I will build my church and the gates of hades will not over-power it."* Hades has gates! Look at what Yeshua said in that verse – "upon this rock." What is this rock? Do you remember? A rock is a stone. What does a stone represent? A stone represents a heart. Upon what rock will Yeshua build His church? Upon the heart... Upon the relationship... Upon His fellowship with us, He is going to build His Church. And do you know what will happen when He builds His church? The gates of hell will not prevail against it!

Two key scriptures are found in Proverbs 24:7 and Psalms 24:7. Both of these scriptures refer to gates, both are in chapter 24, and both are in verse 7, but one is in the book of Psalms and the other is in Proverbs.

> *"Lift up your heads O gates, And be lifted up O ancient doors; That the King of Glory may come in."* (Psalm 24:7)

How do gates lift up their heads? Let me try to give you an illustration here. When you lift up your arms or legs and repeat the motion you are exercising, are you not? A gate is a seat of authority, you are a gate, and therefore you are a seat of authority! Lift up your heads O ye gates = Exercise your authority!

> *"And He called the twelve together, and gave them power and authority over all the demons, and to heal diseases."* (Luke 9:1)

The verse comes alive with, "Lift up your heads O ye gates…" meaning exercise your authority!!

> *"Wisdom is too high for a fool, <u>He does not open his mouth in the gate</u>."* (Proverbs 24:7)

Here we see that if we are not to be called a fool we should open our mouth in the gates.

It would also be good at this point to remind you of Psalm 127:5 which says, *"How blessed is the man whose quiver is full of them; They shall not be ashamed When they <u>speak with their enemies in the gate</u>."*

The Bible makes many references to many different gates. I want to look at these different gates, because it will continue to give you more insight into their significance. Certain events only happened at certain gates. It is important to keep that in mind as you continue to read. Places are important to God. Sometimes, where you are is just as important as what you are doing. You can earnestly be trying to do your best, but if you are in the wrong place, you are not going to get the results you are hoping for. With that in mind, let's look at some gates and at some of the events that occurred at those gates.

The Benjamin Gate

The Bible talks about the Benjamin Gate. *"Pashur had Jeremiah the prophet beaten, and put him in the stocks that were at the upper **Benjamin Gate**, which was by the house of the LORD."* (Jeremiah 20:2) The Prophet Jeremiah was beaten at the Benjamin Gate. It was a place of humbling and humility. Yeshua was also beaten, scourged and humbled. The Benjamin Gate is a place of humility.

The Fish Gate

The Bible talks about the Fish Gate. The image of the fish is a symbol for Christianity. *"Now the sons of Hassenaah built the **Fish Gate**; they laid its beams and hung its doors with its bolts and bars."* (Nehemiah 3:3) The sons of Hassenaah built the Fish Gate. Hassennaah means thorny. Have you ever been a thorn in someone's flesh? Think about it... sometimes, as a Christian, all you need to do is get around unbelievers, or someone with an Anti-Messiah Spirit and you become a thorn to them! Do you remember the crown of thorns that was put on Yeshua's head?

> *"And after weaving a crown of thorns, they put it on His head, and a reed in His right hand, and they kneeled down before Him, and mocked Him, saying, Hail, King of the*

Jews!" (Matthew 27:29)

The Sheep Gate

The Bible talks about the Sheep Gate. *"Then Eliashib the high priest arose with his brothers the priests and built the **Sheep Gate**; they consecrated it and hung its doors."* (Nehemiah 3:1)

> " *Now there is in Jerusalem by the sheep gate a pool, which is called in Hebrew Bethesda, having five porticoes."* (John 5:2)

> *"What man among you, if he has a hundred sheep and has lost one of them, does not leave the ninety-nine in the open pasture, and go after the one which is lost, until he finds it?"* (Luke 15:4)

Eliashib means God will restore. When I was going through a difficult time in my life, right after I had moved from Israel back to the USA, God gave me ONE word – *restore*. At a time when I had lost everything, God spoke that one word, "restore." In the moment when it looked like nothing was working out, I needed to put my trust and hope in Him. I was able to hang on to that word, "Eliashib." It doesn't matter what you have lost, God will restore.

Nehemiah 3:1 tells us that the Sheep Gate was consecrated unto the Lord. Did you know that we are also consecrated unto the Lord? We are the sheep of His pasture. Each of us is important to Him. If even one gets lost, He goes after that sheep until they are restored to the fold. Restoration comes at the Sheep Gate. It doesn't happen at the Water Gate or at the High Gate of Benjamin. He restores at the Sheep Gate. That is where the sheep are restored.

I want you to see the symbolism of the gates. The Bible

talks about a man named, Eliashib at the Sheep Gate. It is a shadow of how God restores the one sheep that has wandered from the fold. Yeshua didn't restore the sheep at the Inspection Gate, and He didn't restore the sheep at the Water Gate. It happened at the Sheep Gate. So there is a place for everything and everything in its place. As you continue this book you will see how things begin to fit together like the pieces of a puzzle.

The Inspection Gate

The Bible talks about the Inspection Gate. God inspects us. We can't hide from Him. He knows where we are and what we are doing – He even knows our thoughts! He inspects our lives and He perfects everything that concerns us. *"After him Malchijah, one of the goldsmiths, carried out repairs as far as the house of the temple servants and of the merchants, in front of the Inspection Gate and as far as the upper room of the corner."* (Nehemiah 3:31) Malchijah means Jehovah is King. The King inspects our lives.

The Valley Gate

The Bible talks about the Valley Gate. *"Moreover, Uzziah built towers in Jerusalem at the Corner Gate and at the **Valley Gate** and at the corner buttress and fortified them."* (2 Chronicles 26:9) Uzziah means my strength is Jehovah. When we are going through the valley, Jehovah is our strength. When we are going through those times when we do not see God, feel God, hear God, and don't even think He is there, He is still carrying us. He is our strength.

The Water Gate

The Bible talks about the Water Gate. The Water Gate is a place that the word was read. Isn't it interesting that Ephesians 5:26 talks about the washing of the water of the word? The water gate was not the gate where the sheep were watered... it was the gate where the Word of God was read. *" And he read from it before the square which was in front of the Water Gate from early morning until midday, in the presence of men and women, those who could understand, and all of the people were attentive to the book of the law."* (Nehemiah 8:3) They were attentive to the book of the law. Where did this occur? Not at the inspection gate. Not at the valley gate. It happened at the water gate. I want you to understand the symbolism of these gates. Understand that they are only a shadow and a type. The Word was read at the water gate.

The Horse Gate

The Bible also talks about the Horse Gate. *"So they seized her, and when she arrived at the entrance of the Horse Gate of the king's house, they put her to death there."* (2 Chronicles 23:15) You die at the horse gate. Well, why would you die there? Why wouldn't you die at the water gate? Water — or the Word — brings life.

"The king is not saved by a mighty army, A warrior is not delivered by great strength. A horse is a false hope for victory, nor does it deliver anyone by its great strength." (Psalm 33:16-17) So here we see death at the Horse Gate. You can't put your trust in horses. It will only lead to death.

"Some boast in chariots, and some in horses; but we will boast in the name of the LORD, our God." (Psalm 20:7) So we see there that we can't put our trust or hope in the strength of a horse, or in the flesh. God wants the flesh to die so that He can live through us. We need to put our trust in the Name of the LORD.

The Old Gate

The Bible talks about the Old Gate. God wants to do a new thing at the Old Gate. The LORD made the Old covenant new. *"Behold, days are coming, declares the Lord,*

*when I will make a new covenant with the house of Israel
and with the house of Judah, not like the covenant which I
made with their fathers in the day I took them by the hand to
bring them out of the land of Egypt, My covenant which they
broke, although I was a husband to them, declares the
Lord."* (Jeremiah 31:31-33)

In this new covenant, God wrote the law upon their
hearts so that they would all know him. So, at the Old Gate
we see that God wants to do something new in our lives.
God is the Creator and He loves to do new things. He is not
going to continue to repeat Himself, and it is important to
know that when it comes to intercession. When I was in the
midst of writing the second portion of the outline for this
current book many people had asked and wanted me to
write down prayers showing them how to go through the
gates. They had asked for examples of prayers. At first, I
didn't want to do it. Because God is so creative, I didn't
want people to pray what the Holy Spirit was putting on my
heart, I wanted them to pray what the Holy Spirit was
putting on their hearts. However, the Holy Spirit had me
write prayers as an example because sometimes when something is a new concept, it helps to have a starting point. You
will find those prayers at the back of this book. I want you
to keep in mind that it's just a starting point. Ask God to
show you how He wants you to pray in every situation.

I always ask God first... Teach me how to pray effectively Holy Spirit. Tell me what is on Your heart. Which
gate would You have me go to today? What is on Your heart
specifically? As you pray, be sensitive to the Holy Spirit and
let Him reveal things to you. It is amazing what He will
show you at the different gates and what He will put on your
heart. You need patience to wait and listen to what He is
saying and then pray it back to him.

The Corner Gate

The Bible talks about the Corner Gate. *"Moreover, Uzziah built towers in Jerusalem at the **Corner Gate** an at the Valley Gate and at the corner buttress, and fortified them."* (2 Chronicles 26:9) Now what does a corner represent? If I am walking and I end up at a corner, I can do one of two things. I have to go one-way or the other. I can't go straight ahead. At a corner, a turn has to be made. So the Corner Gate represented repentance. You are turning. You are changing your mind. You are going in another direction. You also have to fortify that change in direction. In other words, if you are turning from evil, you have to fortify that in order to not go back to what you were involved with before you turned the corner. You need to strengthen or fortify that choice by not falling back into the sinful behavior.

The Dung Gate

The Bible talks about the Dung Gate. I think that gate is self-explanatory. *"Therefore if any man is in Messiah, he is a new creature, the old things passed away; behold, new things have come."* (2 Corinthians 5:17)

The Fountain Gate

The Bible talks about the Fountain Gate. *"Shallum the son of Col-hozeh the official of the district of Mizpah, repaired the Fountain Gate."* (Nehemiah 3:15) Shallum built the Fountain Gate. Repair is taking place at the Fountain Gate. Shallum means "recompense or payment," just like Yeshua paid for us. Yeshua made amends and atonement for us, so that we can have a fountain of life inside of us that will bubble up and move through us.

CHAPTER 7

Where are the Gates?

⚜

A s I began to study and research information on gates, one of the first questions that came to mind was, "Where are gates found in the Bible?"

Gates were found at the city entrance. One of the places gates where found, was at the entrance of a city. *"So he arose and went to Zarepath, and when he came to the gate of the city..."* (1 Kings 17:10)

> *"And he carried me away in the Spirit to a great and high mountain and showed me the holy city, Jerusalem, coming down out of heaven from God, having the glory of God. Her brilliance was like a very costly stone, as a stone of crystal-clear jasper. It had a great and high wall with twelve gates, and at the gates twelve angels, and names were written on them, which are those of the twelve tribes of the sons of Israel."* (Revelation 21:10-12)

In Revelation 21, we see the New Jerusalem coming out

of heaven. It had a high wall, twelve gates, twelve angels stationed at the gates, and the names of the gates were the 12 tribes of Israel. That is really important. That is a key, and we will return to that a little bit later. Isaiah 62:12 says, *"And they will call them the holy people, the redeemed of the Lord, and you will be called a city not forsaken."* So you are called a city. Keep in mind that gates were found at the entrance to a city.

Gates were found at a house. *"And a certain poor man named Lazarus, was laid at his gate, covered with sores..."* (Luke 16:20)

There is a story in Acts 12:14, where Rhoda recognized Peter's voice, but because of her joy, she did not open the gate. Instead she ran inside and announced that Peter was standing in front of the gate. So the gate was at the entrance of the house.

> *"...You also as living stones, are being built up as a spiritual house for a holy priesthood, to offer up spiritual sacrifices acceptable to God through Jesus Christ."* (1 Peter 2:5)

You are called a spiritual house. Gates were found at a house. Gates were found at the entrance of a city, you are called "sought out a city not forsaken."

Gates were found at temples. *"And a certain man who had been lame from his mother's womb was being carried along, whom they used to set down every day at the gate of the temple which is called Beautiful, in order to beg alms of those who were entering the temple."* (Acts 3:2)

Gates were found at a temple. You are called a temple in 1st Corinthians. 3:16 *"Do you not know that you are a temple of God and that the Spirit of God dwells in you?"* (1 Corinthians 3:16)

So far, we have seen that gates were found at the

entrances of a city, at the entrance of a house, and at the entrance of a temple. You are likened to a city, a house, and a temple through the above examples in scripture. *Could you have gates?*

Gates were found at palaces. In the book of Esther 5:9, Haman was seen sitting at the King's Gate. Wouldn't you love to enter through the King's gate? Again we see the King's Gate mentioned in Esther 5:13, *"Yet all of this does not satisfy me every time I see Mordecai, the Jew, sitting at the king's gate."*

Gates were found at camps. *"Now when Moses saw that the people were out of control, for Aaron had let them get out of control to be a derision among their enemies— then Moses stood in the gate of the camp, and said, Whoever is for the Lord, come to me!"* (Exodus 32:25-26)

Where was Moses standing? He was standing at the gate of the camp. Camps had gates. Now camps in the Old Testament were gathering places for war. Have you ever felt as if you were in a spiritual battle or warfare? Everyday we have a choice. When we wake up, we can walk in the spirit or walk in the flesh. We have a battle going on inside – between walking in the flesh, and walking in the spirit. Camps were gathering places for war. If gates were found at houses, and at temples, and at the entrance of a city, and at palaces — and we are likened to all those things in that we are called a spiritual house, a temple, a city — and now we know that gates were found at camps, and camps were gathering places for war ... then guess what? *You are in the Army now!*

Gates were found at rivers. *"The gates of the rivers are opened, and the palace is dissolved."* (Nahum 2:6) The Holy Spirit wants to flow like a river in and through our life. When He begins to flow, the "palace" – or the place of self-centeredness – begins to dissolve. When we diminish, God increases.

Rivers represent the Holy Spirit and living waters.

"If you knew the gift of God, and who it is who says to you, 'Give Me a drink', you would have asked Him, and He would have given you living water..." (John 4:10)

Yeshua likened the Holy Spirit to living waters. Let's talk about the Holy Spirit for a moment. It's important to listen for the voice of the Spirit. Let me give you some examples of the voice of the Holy Spirit. Many times the Lord will tell you to do some things that sound a little strange. When you hear His voice, just do it... obey. He is not going to tell you something that would be contrary to the Word. He is not going to tell you to go out and kill someone... that's not the kind of "strange" I'm talking about. Many times we miss His voice because we do not recognize that the small impressions we get are actually His voice. Sometimes when we get impressions we rationalize and talk ourselves out of doing what the Spirit is prompting us to do. We use our minds and forget that His thoughts are higher than our thoughts. When we hear that still, small, quiet voice, it is critical to move on that impression. You will be amazed at what He will do. Let me give you an example. I was living in Israel in the mid 90's and I was attending Ulpan, which is a place where you learn Hebrew. I attended classes for 5 hours a day. It was very intense. If I missed one day of Ulpan, I missed a lot and had much to make up. One morning on my way to Ulpan the Holy Spirit gave me the impression not to attend classes that morning. I obeyed His voice even though it meant sacrificing a lot by missing a 5-hour day in Ulpan. Instead, He had me do errands and walk around downtown. The entire time I was walking in downtown Jerusalem I was praying and singing in the spirit or in tongues. I was walking and praying. After a number of hours of doing that, on my way home I began to think this was a little bit nuts! That evening I asked the Lord, "Did that singing and praying do anything or make a difference in some way?" Here is what He showed me. That night, there was a terrorist attack in the area that I was walking and praying in. Tragically, 2 people were killed and 13 wounded. However, because of the rain that night, not as many tourists were out. The police found 4 grenades that the pins had been pulled — but none of them had gone off. That's a miracle! Fifty people easily would have been killed if those grenades had gone off. The two terrorists who shot up the street were killed. Thank God for the lives that were spared. This all happened as a result of simple obedience to the voice or impression of the Holy Spirit.

I can think of another example from a time when I was living in Israel. A friend had come to visit for a couple of days. She lived in a different part of the country. This friend wanted to talk with me, yet at the same time, the Spirit of the Lord had come upon me. I was praying in tongues and motioned to them that I could not speak to them right then. Even though this was a friend, God had a hold of me and needed me at that moment. I needed to surrender to Him so that He could accomplish what He wanted to do. It really doesn't matter what anybody else thinks even though you may appear to be rude. You see, the Word declares, "My sheep hear my voice and they follow me." Anyway, I couldn't stop praying in tongues. After I was finished I asked the Lord, "What was that all about?" He doesn't always tell you every time you ask, but on this occasion He spoke to me and said, "You just averted a terrorist attack." The next day, in the paper I read that a plot had been uncovered which entailed kidnapping the Mayor of Jerusalem and blowing up the Jerusalem Mall. The authorities apprehended these terrorists who were plotting this attack just before they could execute their insidious plot.

God wants to use us in these last days. There are so many examples of God's intervening power. If we would call upon His Name and be sensitive to His voice and yield to His Spirit, there is no telling how He would use us. There was another situation where I was shown that there was going to be a premature attack in the northern Galilee area and that it would involve poisonous gas. I told my Pastor. I didn't have the funds to rent a car and go up to the northern Galilee to pray. That particular weekend, the Lord brought 5 intercessors from Brownsville in Pensacola, FL. that stayed at my Pastor's house. My Pastor did not share with them anything that I had told him about what the Lord had shown me. One of the visiting intercessors from Brownsville got the same warning about the premature attack in the northern Galilee. God showed them that if they went up and prayed that the attack would be halted. Those 5 intercessors went up there that same weekend and they averted the terrorist attack by praying in unity there. Again... *"My sheep hear my voice and they follow me."* Some of the things the Spirit reveals to us will not make sense to us in the natural. But your job is only to hear the voice of the Holy Spirit and follow or obey.

One time I was in Haifa, Israel and the Lord only spoke one word to me. That word was London. London? What do you mean? When I returned to the USA after living in Israel, I met a man who happened to have an apartment in a predominantly Jewish part of London. God kept on building on that. Once I was walking in a grocery store in a little town in Florida, and the Spirit of the Lord says, "Wait until you see who you are going to meet in the bakery section." I ended up meeting a couple from England. The Lord kept dropping little hints. Much of the time, God doesn't give us the whole picture. He gives us little impressions. That year, God sent me to London for intercession. I went with another lady. Little did we know that after we had left London, three major evangelists had meetings in England. Those three were Reinhardt Bonnke, Marilyn Hickey, and Roberts Lairdon. They all had outreaches within weeks of one another. After I returned to Florida, I found out that a lady in the church I had been attending went to London with her husband. He was on a business trip and the Lord had impressed her to go along with him. While he was conducting business, she (who was an intercessor) was attending to her Father's business. The point I want to make is that before God will move in a particular area He will bring intercessors into that area.

I want to share some things about corporate prayer. Corporate prayer is so powerful. If we come into unity, God commands the blessing (Psalm 133). When someone is leading out in prayer, support him or her and pray along with them. Think about it… if you are at a gate and you have a battering ram, the battering ram is only going to be as strong as the manpower behind it. If you have 12 people holding on to that battering ram and using it to smash through the gate, you will be a lot more effective than one person trying to do it alone! Obviously, more people working together in unity produces more power. Now, lets take the different intercessors, the musicians, dancers, and singers, as well as the ones who declare the Word of the Lord and use them corporately to go through a gate of a city. Do you see the power in that? Can you see God's Weapons of Mass Deliverance? Individuals come together corporately with a common goal. Under the leadership of the Holy Spirit they bind kings with chains and their nobles with fetters of iron — performing Psalm 149.

Let's go back to the point about Rivers of living water.

> *"He who believes in me, as the Scripture said, 'From his innermost being shall flow rivers of living water.'"* (John 7:38)

"There is a river whose streams make glad the city of God. The holy dwelling places of the Most High." (Psalm 46:4)

Much as a river brings forth life, the Holy Spirit, if not hindered or blocked, will bring forth the fruit of righteousness. We need to learn how to open the gate so the River of Life can flow through our lives and to those who are in our sphere of influence. We need to yield to this wonderful Spirit of the living God. He is with us and desires to lead and guide us in all truth. To God be the Glory, great things He has done!

CHAPTER 8

What Occurred at the Gates?

❧❀❦

God loves the gates! Let's think about all the things the Lord loves. What does the Lord love? He loves his children. He loves souls. He loved the world so much that he gave His only begotten Son. He loves a cheerful giver. He loves righteousness. What else does He love? *He loves the gates.*

> *"His foundation is in the Holy mountains;*
> *the LORD loves the gates of Zion more than*
> *all the other dwelling places of Jacob."*
> (Psalm 87:1)

Have you ever seen that in the Bible before? Why would the Lord love gates? I asked the Lord about it, and I want to share some of what He revealed to me.

In Psalm 87, the word declares that the Lord loves the gates of Zion more than all the other dwelling places of Jacob. Jacob had twelve sons. Those twelve sons were given an inheritance. They all had land, but God said He loves the gates. God loves the gates of Zion. I asked Him, "God, why do you love the gates so much? Why do you love the gates?" What He told me was that He loves the gates because they are the place where His people come into His Kingdom. The gates allow us to come into His Presence. A gate goes two ways. A door swings two ways — in and out. God reaches out the gates, through us, to meet the world. We are His gateway to the world. People get saved at the gate. That's why He loves the gates of Zion more than any other gate. We are His vehicles. We are His instruments. He can come through us to meet other people, just like we go through Yeshua to meet and fellowship with Him. We go through Yeshua to get to the Father and the Father goes through us to get to lost people. The gate swings both ways. God loves the gates!

What occurred at the gates?

Wisdom utters her voice at the gates. *"Wisdom is too lofty for a fool, he does not open up his mouth up at the gates."* (Proverbs 24:7)

Wisdom is knowledge applied. If we have knowledge and do not apply it, we are foolish. Conversely, when we have knowledge and apply it we are wise. For example, if I know that I need to bless the Lord at all times (Psalm 34) and I choose not to bless the Lord, then I am not exercising wisdom. "At all times" mean even when you have no money, when you are sick, when you are disappointed, when you are disillusioned, when you are angry, when you are frustrated, and when you are at the end of yourself. When the word says, "Bless the Lord at all times," it means just that — no matter what the circumstance is Bless the LORD! Let's take this back to Proverbs 24:7; you now know that wisdom is too lofty for a fool, because he doesn't open his mouth at the gates. Wisdom speaks when it sees the enemy at the gates.

Let's look at other scriptures in Proverbs 1:20-21, which states, *"Wisdom shouts in the street, She lifts her voice in the square; At the head of the noisy streets she cries out; At the entrance of the gates in the city, she utters her sayings:"* This whole chapter is talking about wisdom. Wisdom cries out and at the entrance of the gates of the city — she utters her sayings. Who is crying out? Wisdom. Wisdom is crying out. It is wise to utter your voice at the gates.

Courts of Justice were held at the gates. Deuteronomy 16:18 *"You shall appoint for yourselves judges and officers in all of your towns [towns here are literally gates] which the LORD your God is giving you according to your tribes, and they shall judge the people with righteous judgment."*

Courts of justice were held at the gates. God is a just God. Our case can be presented before Him and we can trust in His justice. We can come before God, because He is in covenant relationship with us. His word is true. He says in his Word that He watches over His Word to perform it. He says that He inhabits the praises of His people. He is our salvation. He is our Healer. He is our Deliverer. He is a very present help in time of trouble. As we enter into His gates with thanksgiving and His courts with praise, He inhabits us. If He inhabits us then we are healthy. If He inhabits us then we have more than enough, because one of His names is El Shaddai — the God that is more than enough. He is Jehovah Jireh — the One who sees ahead and makes provision. He is our Provider and knows what our needs are going to be.

Land was redeemed at the gates. Let look at the Lord's Prayer, *"Our Father which art in heaven, hallowed be thy name. Thy kingdom come, thy will be done on earth as it is in heaven."* What does God mean when He says "on earth?" We are made out of dust — earth. Thy kingdom come, Thy will be done on earth — on me — as it is in heaven. Land was redeemed at the gates. You were redeemed at the gate. Yeshua is a gate. When you accepted Him as your Messiah you were redeemed.

Proclamations and declarations were made at the gates. *"Thus the LORD said to me, Go and stand in the public gate through which the kings of Judah come in and go out as well as all of the gates of Jerusalem and say to them. Listen to the word of the Lord, kings of Judah and all Judah, and all inhabitants of Jerusalem who come in through these gates."* (Jeremiah 17:19-20)

God didn't say, "Go to the church, go the synagogue, go to the zoo and proclaim my word." He said, "Go to the public gate, and there, at that gate, proclaim my word."

God's Word is truth and it goes forth and does not return empty or void but it accomplished what it was sent to do. (Isaiah 55:11) God's Word is more powerful than a 2-edged sword. (Hebrews 4:12) A lot of times, people pray the problem and they don't pray according to the Word of God. You need to know what the Bible says about your situation. He watches over His Word (Jeremiah 1:12) to perform it. He doesn't watch over our words to perform them. We are to remind God of His Word. We need to speak His Word. It is wonderful to speak in tongues and pray in tongues, especially when we do not know how to pray; but also one of the keys is the Word of God. One of the weapons of our warfare is the Word of God and we must proclaim that Word at the gate.

Councils of State were held at the gates. *"Now the king of Israel and Jehoshaphat the king of Judah were sitting each on his throne, arrayed in their robes, and they were sitting at the threshing floor at the entrance of the gate of Samaria; all the prophets were prophesying before them."* (2 Chronicles 18:9)

The kings of Judah came in and out of the gates. Governmental authorities, Councils of State, Heads of State all met at the gates. As an illustration, I'd like to tell you a funny story. This is a walking by faith story. I came back into the USA from Israel and the Lord was leading me to

Washington, DC. At that point, I had 16 dollars — I had more than a nickel, so I was prospering, things were looking good, but I did have a plane ticket to go to Washington, DC. Another intercessor that was also going to DC said to me, "Nancy, why don't you make the reservations?" Now this is by faith. I called and began to make hotel reservations for DC. The person whom I was speaking with on the phone must have been a new employee. I remember it was around President's day in February. That person at the hotel told me that because of the President's holiday weekend they were running a special and that the price would be $74 for the entire weekend. This was a great deal because the rooms were usually $224 a night. I reiterated to the employee, "You mean to tell me that the special is $74 for the entire weekend?" He assured me that was the price. I made the reservations for the weekend which was 3 nights for the agreed upon special price of $74. A few days before we were to leave for DC, I called to make sure that the confirmation of the reservations was still in tact. I spoke to a woman who let me know that the reservation, which was being held, was $74 per night. I said, "Listen, he told me $74 for the entire weekend and you need to stand by it." She said, "I'm sorry, but this is the way that it is." So I said, "I want to talk to your boss." When I spoke with her boss, I got the same response. Then I requested to speak to that person's boss, but they were on vacation. So I requested to speak to their boss who was the liaison. When she didn't return my call, I asked to speak with her boss. The next day I spoke with the liaison. The point is that I spoke to the head person in charge. The liaison explained to me that the fellow that made the reservation was new and he made a mistake, but they agreed to honor it. Why? Because, I went to the person who was in charge over all those other workers! It is the same thing in the spirit realm. God is revealing to go to the gates, go to the council of state, go to those that are in charge, and go straight to the strongholds. Don't go to the little subordinate spirits or manifestations of the strongmen. If you want to get results, then you go to the one in charge. They have the authority. You want to pray against the stronghold at the gate and not the manifestation of the stronghold. Remember councils of state were held at the gates, you do not want to pray against the manifestations, it is more important to pray against the stronghold and we will address this in a later chapter.

There are 12 strongholds. There are also 12 Tribes – named after the twelve sons of Jacob. There is a pattern, which we will discover. The number 12 represents governmental authority. In the Bible you will see that Ishmael had 12 sons, or they are called the 12 princes. The number 12 is significant in the Bible.

Public Commendations were made at the gates. *"Her husband is known in the gates, When he sits among the elders of the land."* (Proverbs 31:23)

> *"Give her the product of her hands and let her works praise her in the gates."* (Proverbs 31:31)

What do we do when coming into God's presence? We enter his gates with thanksgiving and his courts with praise. What do we do? We commend him.

The gates were shut at nightfall. Think about this, if you are sleeping, demons cannot operate through you. Perhaps one exception might be in dreams, yet for the most part, a spirit of murder is obviously unable to operate when a person is sleeping. Gates were shut at nightfall. That is why it is wonderful to be able to pray early in the morning because you have less demonic activity going on when you first awake. Demons need a body to operate through. They are disembodied spirits that need a body to express their nature.

Gates were a chief point of attack in war. *"New gods were chosen, then war was in the gates"* (Judges 5:8). If you were going to attack a city, you would go to the entrance of that city and attack that gate, and then you could take the city. Gates were a chief point of attack in war. In the Old Testament battering rams were used to attack at the gates.

> *"Into his right hand came the divination, 'Jerusalem', to set battering rams, to open the mouth for slaughter, to lift up the voice with a battle cry, to set battering rams against the gates, to cast up mounds, to build a siege wall"* (Ezekiel 21:22).

The above scripture also indicates that Battering Rams were used against the gates!

Let's go back to Isaiah 62:12, which says that the holy people of the Lord are called *"sought out, a city not forsaken."* Since we are being likened to a city, do we have natural enemies coming to us with battering rams? Of course not! However, we have an enemy who is battering us daily in our minds with lies, suspicions, with accusations, falsehood and deception. He is battering our minds in our thought life. I have had my mind battered by the enemy and I am sure you have too.

I used to live in Jerusalem for 2 years and I never had a problem with fear. I don't like snakes. One day, I was walking down the street in Jerusalem and a snake slithered down the street right next to me. Did I jump? No, I didn't. You are talking about a person who sometimes would take a glass of water and have my finger under the glass, and would think it was a bug — and I would jump! Yet in Jerusalem, I had no fear. I got back to Jacksonville, Florida and realized that irrational fear is the stronghold over that city. When I came into the city, I came under that fear and I was tormented for months. Irrational fear was influencing me. I would take a shower and see a bump on my leg, and begin to think I was going to have to have the leg amputated. The thought or suggestion came, "Your father's leg had to be amputated so now your leg is going to have to be amputated." I got into so much fear that I would take a shower in the dark because I did not want to see if there was anything wrong with me. Fear... irrational fear and torment ...it's never going to get better ... its always going to be like this... it's hopeless. Those thoughts were battering my mind. The enemy's job is to batter your mind with lies. If you are not getting battered in the mind you are either not recognizing your enemy or you are dead. When we get those suggestions or thoughts, what do we do with them? Do we receive them? Absolutely not, we take those thoughts captive to the obedience of Messiah. The Word of God allows us to pull down those strongholds and fortresses.

I would highly recommend a book written by Liberty Savard called *Shattering Your Strongholds*. God has given us keys. He has given us keys to the Kingdom. The question is... are we using them? This book by Liberty Savard talks about shattering strongholds. Did you know that we can bind our minds to the mind of Messiah? We can bind our wills to the will of God. We can bind our feet to the paths of righteousness. God has ordained for us to walk a specific path. If we bind our feet to path of righteousness, then our steps would be sure and steady.

We can loose and destroy wrong patterns of thinking in our lives. God says to renew our minds with the Word. We can crush wrong ideas that we have, wrong behaviors, wrong attitudes, wrong motivations, and wrong habits with the words of our mouths. We are either ensnared by the words of our mouths or we are blessed by the words of our mouths. God watches over his word to perform it (Jeremiah 1:17). As we speak truth, we walk in life. When we speak death, we walk in misery. Life and death is in the power of the tongue, you will be satisfied with the fruit thereof (Proverbs 18:21). Choose this day whom you shall serve (Joshua 24:15). Are we going to serve Satan? God forbid. We will choose to serve God.

I spent some time in Thomaston, Georgia, at Pleasant Valley Church, which is under the leadership of Pastor Henry Wright. Pastor Wright has a well-known and well-respected healing and deliverance ministry. While I was there, I learned to recognize that spirits could be operating in or through you if you do not break fellowship with them or to fall out of agreement with them. Henry Wright calls these spirits "yucky puckies." If we don't recognize what is operating in and through us we can literally be used to serve Satan and build up his kingdom. That is a horrible thought isn't it? Yet when we allow the enemy to get us into unforgiveness, strife, envy, dissentions, etc. we are choosing to build up the kingdom of darkness. So the enemy does batter us, but God wants us to batter the enemy. That's why He gave us the keys! He gave us His Name! He gave us His Word! He gave us the blood of Yeshua! He gave us praise and worship!

Praise the LORD!
Sing to the Lord a new song,
And his praise in the congregation of the godly ones
Let Israel be glad in his Maker
Let the sons of Zion rejoice in their king
Let them praise His name with dancing;
Let them sing praises to Him with timbrel and lyre,
For the LORD takes pleasure in His people
He will beautify the afflicted ones with salvation.
Let the godly ones exult in glory
Let them sing for joy on their beds.

Let the high praises of God be in their mouth,
And a two-edged sword in their hand,
To execute vengeance on the nations,
And punishment on the peoples;
To bind their kings with chains,
And their nobles with fetters of iron;
To execute on them the judgment written;
This is an honor for all of His godly ones.
Praise the Lord! (Psalm 149)

Why do you think Psalm 149 says, *"Let them sing for joy on their beds?"* Because the joy of the Lord is your strength (Nehemiah 8:10), and if you have that joy you would be out of bed! You would be dancing! You could be doing more than singing. You can't dance in bed. God is just letting you know, "I know you are on your bed, sing to me, and I will give you strength." In the presence of the Lord there is strength, power, and might. In the presence of the Lord there is fullness of joy. The joy of the Lord is your strength...so if you are on your bed *sing to him.*

When you dance, and when you sing, and when you twirl, and you "hallel," you are binding the kings or strong-men with chains. (Psalm 149) Through your high praises you are literally binding up the enemy. It is time that we use the weapons of our warfare, which are mighty through the pulling down of fortresses and strongholds. We need to batter the enemy for a while.

Gates were often razed or burned. Let me share a story with you. Once, I was speaking with a friend who was going to be traveling overseas on a mission trip. I started praying for her. As I did, I saw this wall of fire. I asked her if I could pray for this wall of fire to be around her. With her permission, I continued to pray. In the spirit, I could see this fire above her head and around her. A couple of days after that, the Lord showed me in Zechariah where God was speaking about Jerusalem (you know… we are the New Jerusalem). Zechariah states, *"For I, declares the LORD, will be a wall of fire around her, and I will be the glory in her midst."* (Zechariah 2:5) My point is this; we need to pray for protection, especially before we go into intercession. God is a wall of fire around us and the fiery darts from the enemy can't touch us because they are extinguished. The same principles apply in nature. Firemen will often start a backfire. They fight fire with fire. When the fire they want to extinguish touches the back fire, there is nothing left for fuel – nothing left to burn! This is what extinguishes the destructive fire. If you are going to be burned, let it be with God's fire, which is able to cleanse you and purify you. You will come forth as gold! Don't allow the fire of the enemy to torment you.

We can pray when we enter into intercession, "God be a wall of fire around me! Let your glory be in my midst. Hide me in the cleft of the rock. Put me under the shadow of your wings." Psalm 91 is a Psalm of protection. I recommend that we pray Psalm 91 over ourselves daily — especially in the days we are living in. *"No evil shall befall you, nor will any plague come near your tent. For He will give his angels charge concerning you, to guard you in all of your ways; A thousand may fall at your side, And ten thousand at your right hand; but it shall not approach you. For you have made the LORD my refuge Even the Most High, your dwelling place."*

What is our responsibility? It is to dwell in the secret place of the Most High God. We need to remind God of his Word. As we do that, the angels of the Lord go out and perform the Word. It is important to sow the Word of God in our hearts. David sowed the word of God in his heart so that he would not sin against God. We need to know His Word so that when trials come, we will bless the Lord at all times and have his praise continually in our mouths.

It is essential that head knowledge come into our heart.

It must be more than an intellectual understanding. Embrace God and His word with every fiber of your being. Know that you are a gatekeeper in your city; in your family; in your church; in your region. God has trusted you and given you great power, great authority, and great responsibility. When you hear this revelation and you implement it, you will participate with the Holy Spirit in effecting change in the Kingdom of God. You will restrain the powers of darkness and make a way for the Lord in the wilderness.

When I first began to comprehend this revelation, I struggled with a lot of fear in my life. I began to go to the Gate of Gad. Gad means good fortune and fear happens to attack at the Gate of Gad. The manifestations of fear are anxiety, stress, and worry. One day, I noticed that the name Gad is also the acronym for General Anxiety Disorder (G.A.D.) People who suffer with that anxiety disorder take a medication called, Paxil to cope with the fear and anxiety. But, they could simply bind fear at the Gate of GAD and renew their minds with the Word of God. ***Fear not***! When I was tormented with fear, I would go to the Gate of Gad and bind fear and begin to declare God's Word. My declaration would be, *"The Lord is my light and my salvation whom shall I fear? The Lord is the defense of my life of whom shall I be afraid? When enemies came against me to devour my flesh, my enemies and adversaries they stumbled and fell. Though a host encamps against me, my heart will not fear. Though war rise up against me in spite of this I will be confident."* (Psalm27). What was I doing? Renewing my mind. What else was I doing? Releasing angels to go out and perform the Word of God. The enemy at the Gate of Gad is trying to batter my mind and get me into all the dread, fear, poverty, and everything else that comes with that. God watches over his Word to perform it. How does He do that? Psalm 103:20 says that the angels obey the voice of God's Word. I encourage you, become the voice of God's Word!!

Acts of idolatry happened at the gates. *"And the priest of Zeus, whose temple was just outside of the city, brought oxen and garlands to the gates, and wanted to offer sacrifice with the crowds."* (Acts 14:13)

I was on the internet and I found something intriguing on a site that the Lord had given me permission to go into. I am not going to reveal the site, but it talked about the city of Atlanta, Georgia. Atlanta is nicknamed "a gated city." The website gave all of the information about this particular "sect." I wouldn't call this group a cult, but they gather together and the group is in deception and ungodly. The Lord led me to read the acceptance speech of the high priest in this particular group (which is not a Christian group). They are a group that is very well known throughout the world. They are very organized, but they are in deception. This speech gave all of the information of the history of the organization. It described their history in England. It spoke about a deed, and a warrant. The speech gave dates and a number of things that were pertinent to the organization.

I started to realize that the Lord was releasing much understanding. When the Lord releases information to us, we have to know what to do with that knowledge. If you are an intercessor, and God gives you information, a lot of times you may feel like you have to run with the information. I've done that myself. We run to the Pastor. We start running right away and want to do something with that information! We really need to wait. This is where maturity comes into play.

When the Lord was revealing things to me on this website, the first thing that came to my mind was that I needed to get this to an Apostle in the Atlanta area. God has given each of us authority. Some of us, He has given authority over our families. Some, He has given a local call and authority over a city. Still others, He has given an international call. It is critical to know where and what your boundaries are, because that is the only place you have authority.

At that time, God had given me a boundary of authority. I had a sense that I could go anywhere in the southeastern part of the USA. The boundaries set for me to travel were as far north as Washington, DC and as far west as Dallas/Ft. Worth. Within that area, Atlanta fell. I could have taken the authority and gone to that gate in Atlanta and prayed, however, I did not sense the prompting of the Lord to do that. I felt that I needed to share that information with a spiritual authority in the area. The point is, that you have to be mature enough to know that when the Spirit of the Lord entrusts you with something. Seek Him and find out what He wants you to do with it.

Timing is so critical when dealing with the things of God. Once, God gave me a Word for a Church that I was attending, and it was a powerful Word, however it was delivered prematurely and was not received. Hearts had not been prepared to receive the Word. We can speak things that are truth, but if the people are not ready to receive it, then what good is it? You want to give a Word in due season. You want to go according to God's timing. It is not good to get ahead of God. Be sensitive. Know what God is saying and what He expects you to do with what He has given you. Remember... He leads; we follow.

Experienced officers are placed over the gates. Experienced officers are in authority over the gates. Let me explain that a bit further. The devil is smart. He is not going to offer me crack cocaine because I don't have a problem with crack. Yet he might offer me an M&M. Do you understand what I am saying? He may offer me a piece of pumpkin pie, but he is not going to offer me crack or alcohol because it will not create a problem for me. The devil is smart enough to know my weakness. So what is your weakness? I've got news for you — the **devil knows!** He knows your weakness. He knows how to push your buttons. He will set you up and much of the time you will fall for it! It will continue to happen until you recognize the enemy and say, "No way devil! Get behind me Satan!" The devil really isn't that creative. He will use the same trap every time. Whatever your weakness is... remember, experienced officers are at the gates.

The enemy is organized. The enemy has experienced officers. The enemy has an attack strategy. The enemy has ranks. In the military there are ranks and levels of authority. In the military there are requirements of submission to those in authority of a higher rank and file. It works the same way in the enemy's kingdom. You may see manifestations of a stronghold. If you pray against a manifestation, you can cast out a manifestation, but if you don't go to that stronghold, that demon that was giving you the manifestation can come right back under the higher authority — *and you haven't really accomplished anything!*

The first time I taught this was on Oct. 31 of '99. There was a certain couple in that meeting that caught hold of this very truth – the enemy's rank. They took the Logos Word and it became Rhema to them. Unbeknownst to me, they had a prison ministry. Through their ministry, the captives were being set free because they had the revelation of going to the strongman and not to the lesser demon that was manifesting.

I'll give you a personal example. One morning, I was really restless and I couldn't understand why. I could take authority over a spirit of restlessness if I wanted to, and cast it out, but I sensed that there was something more to what was happening. I decided to call a friend and ask her to pray with me. As soon as I was done talking to her, it was quickened to me to search through my study notes to see what the manifestation of restlessness was. Restlessness manifests at the Gate of Naphtali, but the stronghold that attacks at that gate is jealousy! (I'll explain this more in-depth in the following chapters as you read on) Now, I didn't feel jealous at all. I felt restless. Nonetheless, I bound and took authority over the spirit of jealousy and the restlessness left. Action comes after understanding. We often quote the scriptures, stating that the fervent effectual prayer of a righteous man availeth much. We can be righteous in the eyes of God. We can be very fervent in our prayers, but if we're not *effectual* it's not going to avail much. We're going to talk about those 12 strongholds and the manifestations as we continue. I believe it will completely change the way you pray!

There is another side to this story, however, because God wants to develop you into an experienced officer at the gates! If you've ever read the book, *God's Dream Team* by Tommy Tenney, he makes reference to what he calls "gate keepers." The following is paraphrased from Tommy Tenney's book. This term, gatekeepers, can refer to pastors, intercessors, and virtually anyone who exercises spiritual influence. Even in the secular realm, there are certain professionals, politicians, and influential people whose authority is channeled in and out of a city. Influence is channeled in and out of a city through these gatekeepers. In God's kingdom, you have been assigned as a gatekeeper. As you seek God and meditate in His Word, you will develop into an experienced officer in the army of the Lord. You have power and authority. If we intend to see the spiritual atmosphere of our city change, we must be willing to be spiritual gatekeepers.

Tommy Tenney writes about Jerusalem being a type of a church. This great city had 12 gates, and each gate had a name. Which gate is yours? Do you know where your place is? Do you know who and where the other gatekeepers are? Who will stand – united — in the gates for the city? Remember, the New Jerusalem has 12 gates. The number 12 represents governmental authority.

To make this point clearer, let me quote Tommy Tenney from his book, *God's Dream Team. "So what good does it do if you guard your gate, but I don't guard mine? The city will still be vulnerable because of a lack of unity. If you lock your gate but I refuse to lock mine then there's at least one major entrance into the city that's accessible to the enemy."*

You are a spiritual gatekeeper in your geographical area. You have the ability to allow influence into and out of your city. You don't want perversion in your city. You don't want familiar spirits. You need to be in prayer – asking God, "What are the strongholds over this area? Who are the experienced officers that the enemy has placed at the gates?" It's amazing what God wants to reveal. As we begin to do this, revival is going to break out. God has not forgotten you. Timing and trust are two keys in all of this teaching that I am sharing with you. God's plan for you has to do with the end time revival. It has to do with timing. Trust Him. Timing is so important. I really believe that we are in the end times. This teaching and the revelation that God has given is an end time teaching. If you take a hold of this teaching, it will usher in His glory and His presence in your area of the world – wherever you may be. Isn't that exciting? God calls us to hear His voice and obey, no matter what the cost. Are you willing to obey no matter what the cost? It might cost you a lot. God has said, "I will be your shelter, and I'm causing you to die daily." That's the key. Not my will God, but Yours be done. We need to be asking God how to go through the gates – and be willing to obey – not matter what He tells us.

We need to understand that we are gatekeepers and we can enter through His gates. We enter His gates with thanksgiving and His courts with praise. In order to do that effectively, we have to know who we are. My mentor said to me recently, that God was being very quite about what He was going to do because of 3 things that He wants us to do, first.

1. He wants us to know who we are in Him.
2. He wants us to flow.

3. He wants us to grow.

He wants us to know who we are in Him. He wants us to grow in what He's already shown us and then to flow in it. He wants to mature us into experienced officers in the spirit. We haven't been doing everything that we know to do and one of those things is to enter His gates with thanksgiving and enter His courts with praise.

> *"But you are a chosen race, a holy nation, a people for God's own possession, that you may proclaim the Excellencies of Him who has called you out of darkness into His marvelous light."* (1 Peter 2:9)

That's who you are! You're a royal priesthood. You are a holy nation. You're a peculiar people who have been called out of darkness by Him. You're special! He has chosen you. You have to know that – inside.

I had been an intercessor for a number of years when the LORD began to reveal that scripture in Isaiah 62:10-11 that says, *"Go through, go through the gates, clear the way for the people, build up, build up a highway, remove the stones. Say to the daughter of Zion, Lo your salvation comes."* I knew that it had something to do with intercession but I didn't really understand it at first. If I say to you, "Go through the gates," but you don't really understand what that means, what are you going to do? You're probably just going to stand there. But, if you know what to do, you're going to do it! Action comes after understanding. When God says to us, "Go through, go through the gates," many times we're just standing there because we don't know what to do. All right... "Clear the way for the peoples." Hello? Clear the way for the people. Build up a highway. Remove the stones. As you read on, I want to shed some light, specifically, on what these things mean. If you understand them, then you can put them into action. You can become an authority in them. God can give you keys. Keys can open doors. Keys can give you freedom. Think about somebody in jail. If you give them keys, they can go free. If they've got the keys and they don't do anything with them, they stay in jail. But if you give them the keys and they unlock the doors, they're out! So I can give you keys and I can give you understanding, but if you don't use the keys, you stay in jail and the captives stay in jail in your city. If you grab hold of this understanding and you grab hold of this teaching and you use it and you implement it then we all go free. Glory to God!

CHAPTER 9

The City of God

"Great is the Lord and greatly to be praised, in the city of our God His holy mountain." (Psalm 48:1)

"And He carried me away in the Spirit to a great and high mountain, and showed me the holy city, Jerusalem, coming down out of heaven from God having the glory of God. Her brilliance was like a very costly stone, as a stone of crystal-clear jasper. It had a great and high wall with 12 gates, and at the gates were 12 angels, and names were written on them, which are those of the twelve tribes of the sons of Israel." (Revelation 21:10-12)

I can remember back to a time in my life when I felt so defeated that all I did was lay in bed. I had no victory in my life. One day, I think God looked at me and understood that I was "dead." By that, I mean that He could see that I had come to the end of myself, and I understood that I couldn't do anything in my own strength. I needed Him. When I was ready to get myself out of the way, He was ready to move. God had to wait on me. I was waiting on God, but in reality, *God was waiting on me.* He was waiting for me to die. At the appointed time, He gave me a vision. The vision was the New Jerusalem coming down out of heaven. I heard a voice saying, "Nancy! Go through the gates!" At that time, I had been an intercessor for a number of years. I knew that scripture from Isaiah 62 had to do with intercession — but I didn't yet have the revelation of it. God was saying, "Come to Me! Go through the gates!" The picture that He gave me was the New Jerusalem coming down out of heaven, but I saw spiritual strongholds that would not allow me to get through the gates.

I read that scripture from the book of Revelation about the 12 gates, the 12 tribes, and the names of the gates being the 12 tribes of the sons of Israel. I saw the angels stationed at the gates, and I saw the New Jerusalem — *but I couldn't go through the gates.*

Prompted by what the Lord showed me, I began to research what the meanings of the tribes and their names were, because God was saying, "Go through, go through the gates." Here is what I discovered...

Reuben means *behold the son, behold the Messiah.*
Simeon means *hearing*
Judah means *let God be praised*
Zebulon means *dwelling*
Asher means *happy*
Gad means *good fortune*
Naphtali means my *wrestling*
Dan means *judge*
Issachar means *man of hire*
Benjamin means *son of my right hand*

Joseph means *one who increases*
Levi means *joined or joint heir*

I looked at these names and the Holy Spirit spoke to me. He said, "Go and get the stronghold teaching that you heard at Orlando Christian Center." I had sat under the teaching of Pastor Benny Hinn for a number of years. What the Spirit was referring to was a teaching on strongholds that I had written in my Bible.

Can I say something very important here? How many times have we sat in services and taken notes on bulletins? Where are those notes today? Think about it! Did demons eat them? Many of us could answer, "I have no idea where they are? They're gone." When we go and hear a woman or man of God teach us, we should have a notebook or a journal – an organized way to document the information. God uses everything. He doesn't waste anything. Do you take notes when you hear a message? Are those notes taken on Church bulletins, or in a journal, or do you even take notes? It is important to meditate on your notes of those different messages. God is not speaking to you just to make you happy on Sunday; He is giving you (through his spokesmen and spokeswomen) wisdom! He wants to give you victory for your life. This particular time, as the Spirit spoke to me, I knew I had those notes written in my Bible, so I was able to put them to use.

Remember when Yeshua divided the fish and the bread? How many baskets were left? Twelve. Why twelve? He fed five thousand and had twelve baskets remaining. Twelve is a key number. Make a note of that – twelve is a key number. Twelve is a number of governmental authority. When I looked at my notes from Pastor Benny Hinn's teaching there were twelve strongholds. The Spirit was showing me the connection between the strongholds and the meaning of the names of the twelve tribes. Did they correlate? Yes... they did! Each stronghold from those teaching notes matched up to one of the tribes of Israel. <u>Let me show you how they correlated:</u>

Reuben means *behold the son*. One of the strongholds is the Anti-Messiah (or Anti-Christ) Spirit. What does the Anti- Messiah, or we could say it anti-anointed one want you to do? It wants you to *not* be able to behold the Son; *not* to behold the Messiah; *not* to have that relationship with Yeshua. That is what the Anti-Messiah Spirit does, it separates you from Messiah. This spirit does not want you to be able to behold the Son.

I received further revelation on this spirit during a week I spent in Thomaston, Georgia, at Pleasant Valley Church. Dr. Henry Wright, who is the Pastor at that church, wrote a book called, *A More Excellent Way.* I would highly recommend that you read it. His ministry also teaches on the Anti-Messiah spirit, however, they call it an *unloving spirit*, which makes perfect sense. The most basic and essential instruction that we received from both the Old Testament and the New Testament was to love the Lord your God with all your heart, soul, and might; and to love your neighbor as yourself. Basically, it means to love God, love yourself, and love your neighbor. God is LOVE. The Anti-Messiah Spirit is anti-love. This spirit doesn't want you to love God, love yourself, or love others. It is working to prevent you from receiving and giving God's love, to keep you from loving and accepting yourself, and from loving others.

Simeon means *hearing*. What is the stronghold that would attack at that gate? The Deaf and Dumb Spirit. This spirit wants to keep you deaf to the things of God.

Judah means *let God be praised*. The stronghold that would fight against that gate is Perversion — which produces hatred towards God.

Zebulon means *dwelling*. We are a dwelling place for the Holy Spirit. We are His temple. God wants to dwell with us. He wants to sup with us. He wants to commune with us. We are designed to be His habitation. What stronghold would try and attack at that gate? *Familiar Spirits*. Familiar Spirits also need a habitation to be able to pass through the generations. They want to usurp what belongs to God. They attack at the gate of Zebulon.

Asher means *happy*. What stronghold would want to attack at that gate? A Spirit of Heaviness.

By now, I saw these things lining up and realized that I was receiving revelation. The gates lined up with the strongholds. A light bulb went on in my mind as I realized God was saying to me, "Go through, go through the gates." Since going through the gates would put me in His presence, these strongholds were fighting to keep me out.

Gad means *good fortune*. *"For I know the plans that I have for you, declares the LORD, plans for welfare and not for calamity to give you a future and a hope."* (Jeremiah 29:11) God's plans are good plans for us. What tries to attack the gate of Gad? A Spirit of Fear. Fear gives us negative thinking, filled with doubt, unbelief and dread.

Naphtali means *my wrestling*. Jealousy attacks at this gate. You know, we do not wrestle against flesh and blood but against spiritual principalities and wicked powers in high places. We are not to wrestle horizontally with people, but to wrestle vertically with the spirits who are controlling the people. The enemy tries to get us into wrestling with each other through competition, jealousy, strife, and division to stop us from wrestling with the powers of darkness.

Dan means *judge*. What stronghold would attack at that gate? A Spirit of Bondage. A judge will either set you free or lock you up. Yeshua didn't come into the world to condemn it. He came into the world to save it. (John 3:17) Bondage tries to keep you bound instead of giving you freedom. Where the Spirit of the Lord is, there is liberty. God wants to liberate us. Yeshua came to mend the broken hearted and set the captives free. (Luke4:18)

Issachar means *man of hire*. When you hire a man he becomes your servant. The enemy wants us to serve him. How does Satan get people to serve him? Through a Spirit of Whoredom, which manifests itself through the love of money and love of the world. These are the ways that Satan says, "Serve me. Don't serve God!" The Bible explains that we are to love the Lord with all our heart, all of our strength, and our entire mind. The enemy tries to get us to serve and love the things of the world. The Bible plainly explains that if we love the world and the things of the world that the love of the Father isn't in us. (1 John 2:15)

Benjamin means *son of my right hand*. Yeshua humbled himself and He was exalted to the right hand of the Father. What enemy would attack at this gate? A Spirit of Pride. Pride is in direct opposition to humility.

Joseph means *one who increases or gathers*. When you increase you think about increasing in strength, effectiveness in the kingdom, or even in finances. God is always thinking about increase and multiplication. What does the enemy try to do? Rob you. The method by which he does this is through a Spirit of Infirmity. Think about a healthy plant. It is fruitful and it reproduces. Think about a sick plant. It dies. Infirmity is a robber. Infirmity is designed to make you decrease and diminish — until it kills you.

Levi means *joined or joint heir*. We need to know who we are in Messiah. We are joined together with Yeshua. We are heirs to the kingdom of God. A Lying Spirit attacks at the gate of Levi — trying to convince us who we are *not*.

There are 12 gates representing the 12 tribes of the sons of Israel. There are also twelve strongholds stationed at the gates. There are also angels at the gates. All of this came together as the Holy Spirit was showing me a vision of the New Jerusalem. At that time, I came before the Lord and acknowledged what He was showing me, however, I asked

Him for a scriptural reference. Basically, I told the Lord, "I need something to back this up, (that is that there were 12 strongholds at the gates as well) because I don't want to go outside of the Word." I didn't want to teach heresy and God knew that. We need to know that what we believe God is showing us is not just our imagination. In order to do that, we need to base everything on what His Word says. I asked the Lord to give me a reference to show that these strongholds are also at the gates.

> *"Then he said to me, Son of man, raise your eyes, now, toward the north. So I raised my eyes toward the north, and behold, to the north of the altar gate was the idol of jealousy at the entrance."* (Ezekiel 8:5)

This confirmed what the Lord had shown me. Angels are stationed at the gates and strongholds are stationed at the gates. God was saying, "Go through, go through the gates. Clear the way for the peoples. Build up, build up a highway, remove the stones." You also need to keep in mind that strongholds are there at the gates, and they have to be dealt with.

In Psalm 127:5 we are encouraged to speak to the enemy at the gate. *"How blessed is the man whose quiver is full of them; They shall not be ashamed, When they speak with their enemies in the gate."*

Earlier, we looked at the scripture that says, *"wisdom utters her voice at the gates."* (Proverbs 1:21) We must speak to the enemy at the gates. Now, don't just speak anything... Speak wisdom from God's Word. This is because the angels are watching over God's word to perform or act it out in response to our prayers and declarations. (Jeremiah 1:12) Our words will activate the angels to arrest (so to speak) the strongholds who are keeping us out of God's presence. Once that happens, we enter in through the gates. If we speak our words – instead of God's Word — or we complain or murmur, then the angels just stand there! They are actually waiting for us to come into agreement with the Word of God. Once we do, they are able to assist us. They are ministering angels and warring angels, whom are assigned to us. I encourage you to keep your angels busy by declaring and proclaiming the Word of God. We are the gatekeepers in our cities. How do we guard our cities? We speak to the enemy at the gate. You have been given the authority and the angels are waiting for you to exercise that authority so they can perform their duties.

> *"Then the Lord said to me, You have seen well, for I am watching over My word to perform it."* (Jeremiah 1:12)

> *"Bless the LORD, you His angels, Mighty in strength, who perform His word, Obeying the voice of His word!"* (Psalm 103:20)

As we declare His word the angels obey the voice of His word. You are the voice of His word!

CHAPTER 10

Enemy at the Gate

✦

As we move ahead, I'm going to be restating some of the truths we have previously discussed, and also bring more elements into the picture. It is important to keep in mind that Worship is your key weapon. God is raising up Worshipers, Musicians and Dancers in this generation to unleash waves of deliverance, waves of God's love, and waves of His undeniable presence. God dwells in the praise of His people. As you read further, ask God to develop the weapon of worship within you, and to show you how to apply these principles in your worship. With that in mind, let's talk more in depth about the 12 gates.

Gate of Reuben
Attacking Stronghold: Anti-Messiah Spirit
Key: The blood of Yeshua

Reuben means *behold the son*. The Anti-Messiah Spirit attacks at this gate. It doesn't want you to recognize your Messiah. To illustrate this more clearly, I want to tell you a story. I bought a certain young boy that I know a Veggie

Tales videotape. It's important to tell you that this boy is Jewish, and so are his parents. I found through observation, that this family was greatly influenced by the Anti-Messiah Spirit, very much in the same manner as I was before I was saved. I gave this boy the tape. It was a great tape — just wonderful — on the story of Esther. It had nothing to do with Yeshua or Christianity. It was only on the book of Esther from the Old Testament, which the Jewish people believe in. I didn't think that I was doing anything wrong by giving him this tape. Knowing their sensitivity, I looked very carefully over the tape cover to make sure that there was nothing about Yeshua— nothing about Jesus – the cover was only about Mordecai and Esther. After I presented the gift, this boy's mother found an insert on the inside of that tape. Please understand, when I purchased and presented the videotape, it was shrink wrapped, however, on a paper insert, inside of the shrink-wrapped package, in very small print, there was a sentence that said, "You can buy these tapes at any Christian bookstore." This mother aggressively confronted me. She wouldn't allow her son to have the tape. This was a tape about Esther, but because I didn't have x-ray vision and couldn't see that little insert inside of the package, she wouldn't receive the gift. In fact, she started a big fight. She said, "You are always pushing this down our throats." Think about the intensity of this type of a response, all sparked by a few printed words that were so small you nearly needed a magnifying glass to see it. The spirit that had control of her was an Anti-Messiah Spirit.

An Anti-Messiah Spirit wants to kill the Messiah in you. One of the keys that the Lord showed me about this gate was in applying <u>the blood of Messiah</u>. We overcome the enemy by the blood of the lamb, and the word of our testimony and we did not love our lives even unto death. (Revelation 12:11) Speaking about the blood of Yeshua is a powerful weapon to defeat the enemy.

Anti-Messiah Spirit attacks the Gate of Reuben

"...and every spirit that does not confess Jesus is not from God; and this is the spirit of the antichrist, of which you have heard that it is coming, and now it is already in the world." (1st John 4:3)

Manifestations of an Anti-Messiah Spirit

Legalism   Against Messiah
Blasphemies   Persecution of the saints
Controlling spirit   Super spiritual ministries
Opposing men of God   Humanism
Substituting the blood   Atheism
Speaking against the gifts New age
Self-appointed

Gate of Simeon
Attacking Stronghold: Deaf and Dumb Spirit
Key: Fasting

Simeon means *hearing*. The Deaf and Dumb Spirit attacks at this gate.

> *"And one of the crowd answered Him, Teacher I brought You my son, possessed with a spirit which makes him mute;*
>
> *And whenever it seizes him, it dashes him to the ground and he foams at the mouth, and grinds his teeth, and stiffens out. And I told Your disciples to cast it out, and they could not do it.*

And he answered them and said, O unbelieving generation, How long shall I put up with you? Bring him to Me!

And they brought the boy to Him. And when he saw Him, immediately the spirit threw him into a convulsion, and falling to the ground, he began rolling about and foaming at the mouth.

And he asked his father, How long has this been happening to him? And he said, From childhood.

And it has often thrown him both into the fire and into the water to destroy him. But if you can do anything, take pity on us and help us!

And Jesus said to him, If you can, All things are possible to him who believes.

Immediately the boy's father cried out and began saying, I do believe; help my unbelief.

And when Jesus saw that a crowd was rapidly gathering, He rebuked the unclean spirit, saying to it, You deaf and dumb spirit, I command you, come out of him and do not enter him again.

And after crying out and throwing him into terrible convulsions, it came out; and the boy became so much like a corpse that most of them said, He is dead!

But Jesus took him by the hand and raised him; and he got up.

And when He had come into the house, His disciples began questioning Him privately, Why could we not cast it out?

And He said to them, This kind cannot come out by anything but prayer and fasting."
(Mark 9:17-29)

This gate is the place to pray for someone's salvation. Think about it. This Deaf and Dumb Spirit would throw the little boy into the fire or water for destruction. Who wants to throw people into the fire for destruction? Satan.

When a Deaf and Dumb Spirit is operating, the person who is being influenced by this spirit can know the truth, and still refuse to believe it. I have witnessed a Jewish woman listen to the reading of Isaiah 53. I've heard that same Jewish woman say that Isaiah 53 is talking about Yeshua, but that they would never believe in Him. So even while they were saying they understood that the text was describing Yeshua, *they still refused Him!* This is an example of a Deaf and Dumb Spirit at work. Here is key to remember, that God's Word goes out and does not return to him void without accomplishing what it was sent to do. The Word will succeed in the matter for which it was sent. *Fasting is another key in going through the gate of Simeon.*

Deaf and Dumb Spirit attacks the Gate of Simeon

"And one of the crowd answered Him, Teacher, I brought You my son, possessed with a spirit which makes him mute; and whenever it seizes him, it dashes him to the

ground and he foams at the mouth, and grinds his teeth and stiffens out. And I told Your disciples to cast it out and they could not do it." (Mark 9:17)

"And it has often both thrown him into the fire and into the water to destroy him... And when Jesus saw that a crowd was rapidly gathering He rebuked the unclean spirit, saying to it, 'You deaf and dumb spirit, I command you, come out of him and do not enter him again." (Mark 9:22;25)

Manifestations of Deaf & Dumb Spirit

Suicide	Blindness
Convulsions	Eye disease
Epilepsy	Dumbness
Seizures	Deafness
Schizophrenia	Tearing
Lunatic	Foaming mouth
Insane	Pining away
Ear disease	Can't function

Gate of Judah
Attacking Stronghold: Perversion
Key: Holiness

Judah means *let God be praised*. When God is praised, He inhabits the praises of His people. *"God is known in Judah, his name is great in Israel. And His tabernacle is in Salem his dwelling place also is in Zion."* (Psalm 76:1-2) The verse is saying that God is known in Praise. The stronghold that attacks here is Perversion. Perversion causes a twisting of the truth, hatred towards God, and wounds people's spirits. When I first got saved, I believe a spirit of perversion was operating because my thought process was twisted. Do you know how John 3:16 says that God so loved the world that he gave his only begotten son? Well, I was thinking if Yeshua was perfect and God allowed Him to go through all of that suffering, what was God going to do to me in that I was (and am) imperfect. That is perverted thinking.

Perverted thinking made me think about the fact that Yeshua was here on the earth. He was perfect. He walked a perfect life and God still allowed him to die on a cross. My thinking was steeped in performance orientation. I had no understanding of mercy or grace. I thought if this is the way God the Father treated a perfect Son, then there is no hope for me.

Perversion attacks the Gate of Judah

*"The LORD has mixed within her a **spirit of distortion;** They have led Egypt **astray** in all that it does, As a drunken man staggers in his vomit."* (Isaiah 19:14)

*"He who walks in his uprightness fears the LORD, but he who is **crooked in his ways** despises Him."* (Proverbs 14:2)

"A soothing tongue is a tree of life, But perversion in it crushes the spirit." (Proverbs 15:4)

"But Saul, who was also known as Paul, filled with the Holy Spirit, fixed his gaze upon him, and said, "You who are full of all deceit and fraud, you son of the devil, you enemy of all righteousness, will you not

cease to make crooked the straight ways of the Lord?" (Acts 13:9-10)

Manifestations of Perversion

Twist truth	Homosexuals
Doctrinal error	Lust
Wrong Teaching	Pervert the gospel
Hatred of God	Rebellion
Wounded spirit	Hate
Self-lovers	Error
Sex troubles	

Gate of Asher
Attacking Stronghold: Spirit of Heaviness
Key: Praise

Asher means *happy*. The joy of the Lord is our strength. In God's presence is fullness of joy. (Jeremiah 31:13) The enemy that attacks at this gate is a Spirit of Heaviness. This spirit wants to put gloom and doom on you. Have you ever felt it... heavy, heavy, heavy, hopelessness. Have you ever been trying to get into His presence and heaviness is right there trying to keep you out of His presence. How do you break through? God gives you a garment of praise for a spirit of heaviness. (Isaiah 61:3) You break through with praise. You enter his gates with thanksgiving and his courts with praise. Hallelujah.

Spirit of Heaviness attacks the Gate of Asher

*"To grant those who mourn in Zion, Giving them a garland instead of ashes, The oil of gladness instead of **mourning**, The mantle of praise instead of a **spirit of***

fainting." (Isaiah 61:3)

Manifestations of Heaviness

Self-pity	Despair
Rejection	Discouragement
Sorrow	Mourning
Sadness	Troubles
Hopelessness	Gluttony
Grief	Idolatry
Loneliness	Depression
Gloominess	

<u>Gate of Zebulon</u>
Attacking Stronghold: Familiar Spirits
Key: Repentance

Zebulon means *dwelling place*. We are a dwelling place for the Holy One of Israel. God desires to tabernacle with us.

> *"Or do you not know that your body is a temple of the Holy Spirit who is in you, whom you have from God and that you are not your own?"* (1st Corinthians 6:19)

Familiar Spirits want to usurp the place that is really reserved for God, Himself. A Familiar Spirit is an unclean spirit that is looking for a dwelling place or a habitation.

> *"Now when the unclean spirit goes out of a man it passes through waterless places seeking rest and does not find it. Then it says, 'I will return to my house from which I came'; and when it comes, it finds it unoccupied,*

swept, and put in order. Then it goes, and takes along with it seven other spirits more wicked than itself, and they go in and live there; and the last state of that man becomes worse than the first. That is the way it will also be with this evil generation." (Matthew 12:43-45)

Boy, if you are going to get deliverance in one area you had better fill yourself with the opposite. Otherwise that spirit is going to get 7 others like it and you will be in a worse state. If you are getting free from jealousy you need to fill yourself with love. Be wise if you are in a deliverance ministry or session. Don't do anyone any favors by casting out a spirit if they are not going to be able to keep their deliverance. It will only be more difficult for them when 7 more come back to indwell them.

Familiar Spirits attack the Gate of Zebulon

"Then Saul said to his servants, Seek for me a woman who is a medium, that I may go to her and inquire of her. And his servants said to him, Behold, there is a woman who is a medium at Endor." (1st Samuel 28:7)

Manifestations of Familiar Spirits

Occult	Music beats
Fortune telling	Smells/incense
Horoscope	Witchcraft
Astrology	Hypnosis
New age	E.S.P.
Divination	Psychic ability
Demons/sounds	

Gate of Gad
Attacking Stronghold: Spirit of Fear
Key: Faith

Gad means *good fortune*. Jeremiah 29:11 states that the plans that God has for us are for our welfare and not for calamity. God's plans are to give us a future and a hope. Fear attacks at the gate of Gad. Fear wants to deceive us, get us all stressed out and worried about things. As a man thinks in his heart so is he. If you start thinking fear, anxiety, negative thinking, and stress you are going to become just that. If you think healthy, you will be healthy. If you think sick, you will be sick. If you think prosperous and walk in God's principles, you will be prosperous. How do we change our thinking? We renew our minds.

> *"Finally brethren, whatever is true, whatever is honorable, whatever is right, whatever is pure, whatever is lovely, whatever is of good repute, if there is any excellence, and if anything worthy of praise, let your mind dwell on these things."* (Phil. 4:8)

Why would we ever think about things that are not true? Why would we think that God doesn't love us? Why would we think that He doesn't care about us? Why would we think that life is never going to change? Why would we think those things? There are times when we can be our own worst enemy. Why would we think things like... "This has always happened in my family... this always happens to me, and it will always continue?" We need to renew our minds and find freedom. Faith is the key to overcome fear.

Spirit of Fear attacks the Gate of Gad

"For God has not given us a spirit of timidity, but of power, love, and of discipline." (2nd Timothy 1:7)

Manifestations of Fear

Torment	Inadequacy
Heart problems	Tension stress
Horror	Timidity
Poverty	Nightmares
Worry	Sense Danger
Cancer	Think the worst
Anxiety	Heights
Inferiority	

Gate of Levi
Attacking Stronghold: Lying Spirit
Key: The Word of God

Levi means *joint heir*. Through deception the enemy will plant lies in our minds so that we won't know who we are in God. God's Word says that if we abide in Him and His Word abides in us we will know the truth and the truth will set us free. (John 8:31)

Once, I was listening to a tape of Jack Hayford. He was teaching about the Holy Spirit being the Counselor. When people come to counseling sessions with Jack Hayford, he has them pray in tongues for a little while to let the Holy Spirit reveal and bring to the surface the root of their problem. While I listened to that tape, I was set free of an issue by doing just what he spoke about. Here is what happened, there was a time where I couldn't look at myself in the mirror. I hated myself. I kept on asking God, "Why do I hate myself so much?" I got on my knees and began to pray in the spirit and the Holy Spirit brought a memory to my mind. In this memory, my father was coming after me with his fist and my mother was standing in between my father and myself. I could hear her yelling. No! Don't! At that point, the Holy Spirit said to me," How did you feel about your father right then?" I said, "I hated him. I really hated him." Then the Holy Spirit said, "What has your mother always said about you?" For the first time, I consciously realized that she used to say, "You are just like your father." Instantly, the truth was revealed. I understood why I hated myself. You see I had believed a lie. Here is how the Lord set me free. He said, "You know what, Nancy? You are just like your Father. I am your Father." God started to declare his attributes, and then said again, "You are just like me." From that day on, I did not hate myself anymore. The truth set me free.

Sometimes, we are "locked" into a certain position in life, because we don't fully see and understand the truth. We don't have to stay there. If we abide in Him and His Word abides in us, we will know the truth and it will set us free. Yeshua came to mend the brokenhearted and set the captives free. Psalm 107 states that God sent His Word to heal us and deliver us from all our destructions. The key to get through the gate of Levi is found in the Word!

Lying Spirit attacks the Gate of Levi

"Then they cried out to the LORD in their trouble; He saved them out of their distresses. He sent His word and healed them, And delivered them from their destructions." (Psalm 107:19-20)

"Now therefore, behold, the LORD has put a deceiving spirit in the mouth of these your prophets; for the LORD has proclaimed disaster against you." (2nd Chronicles 18:22)

"Also among the prophets of Jerusalem I have seen a horrible thing: The committing of adultery and walking in falsehood; And they strengthen the hands of evildoers, So that no one has turned back from his wickedness. All of them have become to Me like Sodom and her inhabitants like Gomorrah." (Jeremiah 23:14)

Manifestations of a Lying Spirit

Homosexuality	Superstition
Adultery	Divination
Vanity	Witchcraft
Condemnation	Hypocrisy/delusion
Fornication	Religious spirit
Sodomy	Exaggeration
Profanity	

Gate of Naphtali
Attacking Stronghold: Spirit of Jealousy
Key: Love

Naphtali means *my wrestling*. Our struggle is not against flesh and blood but against principalities and powers.

"For our struggle is not against flesh and blood, but against the rulers, against the powers, against the world forces of this dark-

*ness, against the spiritual forces of wicked-
ness in the heavenly places."* (Ephesians 6:12)

A Spirit of Jealousy attacks the Gate of Naphtali

The enemy tries to get us to fight with each other by creating competition and strife. I hear many people say that they are praying for unity, but if we are going to effectively pray for unity we need to pray against the very spirit that divides. That spirit is Jealousy. The key to overcoming jealousy is to love one another.

> *"If a spirit of jealousy comes over him and he is jealous of his wife when she has defiled herself, or if a spirit of jealousy comes over him and he is jealous of his wife when she has not defiled herself."* (Numbers 5:14)

> *"For jealousy enrages a man, And he will not spare in the day of vengeance."* (Proverbs 6:34)

Manifestations of a Spirit of Jealousy

Rage	Restlessness
Murder	Cruelty
Adultery	Selfishness
Suspicion	Divination
Competition	Wrath
Revenge	Envy

Gate of Issachar
Attacking Stronghold: Spirit of Whoredom
Key: Giving

Issachar means *man of hire*. Now a man of hire is a servant. In this case we are servants of the Most High God. Remember, no one can serve two masters.

> *"No one can serve two masters; for either he will hate the one and love the other, or he will hold to one and despise the other. You cannot serve God and mammon."* (Matthew 6:24)

The demonic power that attacks at the Gate of Issachar is Whoredom. Whoredom tries to get you to serve mammon – to serve money — and not God. The love of money is the root of all evil. (1 Timothy 6:10) If you love the world and the things of the world the love of God is not in you! The key to getting through the gate of Issachar is to give cheerfully. (1 Corinthians 9:7)

> *"For the love of money is a root of all sorts of evil, and some by longing for it have wandered away from the faith, and pierced themselves with many a pang."* (1st Timothy 6:10)

> *"Let each one do just as he has purposed in his heart; not grudgingly or under compulsion; for God loves a cheerful giver."* (2nd Corinthians 9:7)

Whoredom attacks the Gate of Issachar

"Moreover, you played the harlot with the Assyrians because you were not satisfied; you even played the harlot with them and were still not satisfied." (Ezekiel 16:28)

Manifestations of Whoredom

Unclean/foul	Love of the world
Idolatry	Love of money
Homosexuality	Pornography
Fornication	All sexual sin
Prostitution	Emotionally weak
Adultery	Unequally yoked

Gate of Benjamin
Attacking Stronghold: Pride
Key: Humility

Benjamin means *son of my right hand.* This has to do with Yeshua humbling Himself and then being exalted to the right hand of the Father. Sitting at the right hand is an idiom meaning "having authority." Pride is the stronghold that attacks at this gate. The opposite of humility is pride. God is opposed to the proud but he gives grace to the humble. (James 4:6) Pride goes before destruction and a haughty spirit before stumbling. (Proverbs 16:18) As with any one of the gates, we should be asking God to search our hearts and see if there is any unclean way in us and lead us in an everlasting way. If your desire is to be effective for the kingdom, you must take the log out of your own eye before you take the speck out of your brothers' eye. You will not be able to pray effectively about any stronghold at any level if you don't first come out of agreement with that stronghold in your own life. At this gate, we need to ask God to reveal ways in which we have acted with pride. The key to get through the gate of Benjamin is humility.

Spirit of Pride attacks Gate of Benjamin

"Pride goes before destruction, And a haughty spirit before stumbling." (Proverbs 16:18)

Manifestations of Pride

Stubbornness	Mockery
Gossip	Scorner
Control spirit	Egotistic
Arrogance	Haughtiness
Self-righteousness	Proud
Contention	Vanity
Wrathful	Dictatorial

Gate of Dan
Attacking Stronghold: Spirit of Bondage
Key: The Holy Spirit

Dan means *judge*. A Spirit of Bondage attacks this gate. A judge has the authority to set you free or lock you up. As God's children, we can come boldly before Him, as our righteous Judge, and we can remind him of His Word. God wants us to remind Him of His Word. We must have a working knowledge of His Word in order to stand on what is rightfully ours.

Have you ever had anything stolen from you? Do you know what the Word says about that? It says, that if the thief were found out, he has to restore seven times what has been stolen. You can go before your righteous judge at the gate of Dan and boldly remind God of His Word. Fully expect to see the Lord answer your prayers! Why can you expect that? God watches over His Word to perform it. The angels obey the voice of God's Word, and God honors His Word above his name. Any spirit that would attempt to take us into bondage is not from God. God has given us the Holy Spirit who leads us and guides us into all truth. The key to get through the gate of Dan is to listen to the voice of the Holy Spirit.

Bondage attacks the Gate of Dan

"For you have not received a spirit of slavery leading to fear again, but you have received a spirit of adoption as sons by which we cry out, Abba! Father!" (Romans 8:15)

Manifestations of Bondage

Compulsive	Prayerlessness
Addictions	Abused
Cigarettes	Broken
Alcohol	Anguish
Drugs	Lust
Satanic activity	Bitterness
Unforgiving	Greed
Spiritual blindness	Cancer

<u>Gate of Joseph</u>
Attacking Stronghold: Spirit of Infirmity
Key: Worship

Joseph means *one who gathers or increases*. This is where the Spirit of Infirmity attacks. This stronghold has been set up to decrease your effectiveness in the Kingdom of God. It tries to rob you. If the enemy can get you into fear (which is sin), this will bring about many adverse changes in your body, which has the ability to unleash a plethora of illnesses. In addition, God will not be able to hear you if you regard iniquity in your heart.

> *"If I regard wickedness in my heart, The LORD will not hear;"* (Psalm 66:18)

The Word of God instructs us to turn from evil, bringing health to our body and nourishment to our bones. In order to be effective in the kingdom we need to be healthy and have strength. The key to get through the Gate of Joseph is Worship.

Spirit of Infirmity attacks at the Gate of Joseph

> *"And behold, there was a woman who for eighteen years had had a sickness caused by a spirit; and she was bent double, and could not straighten up at all. And when Jesus saw her, He called her over and said to her, Woman, you are freed from your sickness."* (Luke 13:11-12)

116

Manifestations of Infirmity

All sickness
Cancer
Heart
Asthma
Arthritis
Sinus
Ears
Viruses

Colds
Fever
Weakness
Hunchback
Lungs
Bones
Muscles

CHAPTER 11

Gates of Prayer

꧁꧂

As you have read through this book, you may have a new awareness of areas where you may personally need deliverance, or there may be places where the Lord is showing you ways to intercede for geographical areas, cities, and even nations. With all of that in mind, I want to give you some practical ways to begin the application of this information. On the pages that follow, I have included prayers at each of the twelve gates. Please understand that the only reason I wrote out prayers is because some friends of mine who were intercessors wanted examples of how to pray at the gates. I did not want to do this because, as you listen to the Holy Spirit, He is truly the one to direct you. Sometimes you may sing a song at the gate, sometimes dance or declare a particular scripture... remember these are only examples. I believe in Liberty Savaard's Books she calls them "training wheel prayers." As you begin to pray along these lines, I believe the Holy Spirit will begin to give you insight and wisdom on how to pray strategically and effectively in any and every situation — and start to exercise a new level of authority as a child of the Most High God.

Praying at the Gate of Reuben
Attacking Stronghold: Anti-Messiah Spirit
Key: The Blood of Jesus

Father, You are my God and You are my King. I bless You today and I thank You that You have revealed Yourself to me. As I come before You, I apply the blood of Yeshua to my family, my future, my finances and myself. Through the blood of Jesus, You have made my sins that were scarlet, as white as snow. I thank You that You have taken off my filthy rags and clothed me with robes of righteousness. I have nothing to offer You this day but my praise and my love for You. I know that apart from You, I can do nothing. I ask You to fill me with Your presence today, Lord. You told me that it is wise to speak to the enemy at the gate, so I come before the Gate of Reuben and I bind an Anti-Messiah Spirit from operating in my life, my family's lives, my church, our public schools, or in our government. Holy Spirit, help me to behold the Son of righteousness today. The Word says that as I behold Him, I will become like Him. Cause me to walk in Your ways and be obedient to Your commandments. I don't want "religious" activity today Lord, I want You! It is not by power, nor by might, but by Your Spirit – Your yoke is easy and light. I know that Your thoughts and Your ways are higher than mine. Teach me Your ways Lord – lead and guide me. Father, if I have acted legalistically in any way, open my eyes. Lead me in liberty and freedom. You said, Where the Spirit of the Lord is, there is liberty. I desire to worship you alone. Thank You for the Blood of Jesus. Thank You for cleansing me and making me acceptable through Your Son, Jesus. Help me to accept my weaknesses, that I may also accept Your grace and extend it to those who do not know You and myself. Lord I want to lift up the Jewish people and all people who do not yet acknowledge you as Messiah. I speak to the Anti-Messiah Spirit, and bind him according to Your Word. The blood of Yeshua is against you, Anti-Messiah Spirit. Father, I bind the mind of the Jewish people to the mind of Messiah; their wills to the will of the Father; and their lives to the plan and purpose of God. Through the Word, You spoke and said, "All of Israel will be saved. I will be your God, and you shall be My people. Because you are precious in My sight, I will give other men in exchange for your life." Lord, You came for the lost sheep of the house of Israel. Reveal Yourself to Your people for Your Name's sake. Do not forget Your covenant to bless those who bless Israel and curse those who curse Israel. I speak blessings to Israel in Jesus' Name, Amen.

Declarations at the Gate of Reuben/ Anti-Messiah Spirit

2nd JOHN 7-9
"For many deceivers have gone out into the world, those who do not acknowledge Jesus Christ as coming in the flesh. This is the deceiver and the antichrist. Anyone who goes too far and does not abide in the teaching of the Christ, does not have God; the one who abides in the teaching, he has both the Father and the Son."

MATTHEW 24: 23-24
"Then if anyone says to you, 'Behold here is the Christ', or 'There he is', do not believe him. For false Christs and false prophets will arise and show great signs and wonders, so as to mislead, if possible even the elect."

JOHN 10:10-11
"The thief comes but to steal, and kill, and destroy. I came that they might have life and

might have it abundantly."

MATTHEW 11:28-30

"Come to me, all you who are weary and heavy-laden, and I will give you rest. For my yoke is easy, and my load is light."

JOHN 15:18-20

"If the world hates you, know that it hated me before it hated you. If you were of the world the world would love its own; but because you are not of the world, but I chose you out of the world, therefore the world hates you. Remember the word that I said unto you, A slave is not greater than his master. If they persecuted me they will also persecute you;"

JOHN 16:1-3

"These things I have spoken to you, that you may be kept from stumbling. They will make you outcasts from the synagogue, but an hour is coming for everyone who kills you to think that he is offering service to God. And these things they will do, because they have not known the Father or me."

MATTHEW 5:11-12

"Blessed are you when men cast insults at you, and persecute you, and say all kinds of evil against you falsely, on account of me. Rejoice, and be glad, for your reward in heaven is great, for so they persecuted the prophets who were before you."

2nd CORINTHIANS 4:8-9
"...we are afflicted in every way, but not crushed; perplexed but not despairing, persecuted but not forsaken, struck down but not destroyed;"

MATTHEW 5:44a
"But I say to you, love your enemies, and pray for those who persecute you."

MARK 3:27
"But no one can enter the strong man's house and plunder his property unless he first bind the strong man, and then he will plunder his house."

ECCLESIASTES 1:9
"That which has been is that which will be, And that which has been done is that which will be done. So, there is nothing new under the sun."

Praying at the Gate of Simeon
Attacking Stronghold: Deaf and Dumb Spirit
Key: Fasting

Father, in Yeshua's Name, I ask You to hide me in the cleft of the rock. I thank You for being a wall of fire around me. I apply the blood of Messiah within me, upon me, between all evil, and me and between me and the author of all evil. I speak the blood of Yeshua over _____, _____, and _____. Lord, I know you watch over Your Word to perform it. Thank You that You are a God who hears and sees all and even knows the hairs on my head. Psalm 91 states that He who dwells in the secret place of the Most High shall abide under the shadow of the Almighty. I will say to the Lord, You are my refuge and my fortress, my God in Whom I trust. You will cover me with your pinions and under your wings I will seek shelter. No evil will befall me nor will any plague come nigh my dwelling place.

Lord, I come to You at the gate of Simeon on behalf of the unsaved loved ones, unsaved friends, unsaved people in my community and country, and on behalf of the Jews who do not yet recognize you as Lord. Lord, I know that You are not willing that anyone would perish, but that each one would have eternal life. I stand at this gate and speak to the Deaf and Dumb Spirit which would keep people in darkness, and I command that Deaf and Dumb Spirit to be bound from _____'s life. The blood of Yeshua Ha Machiach is against you. Lord, you taught that some spirits only come out by prayer and fasting. I ask you to give me the grace to fast, and I ask you to join my prayers with others around the world that are fasting and praying for new births in the body of Messiah, and salvation to the Jewish people. If You be lifted up, You will draw all men unto Yourself. I lift You up this day, Lord and I thank You that You will draw all men to Yourself. You alone are highly exalted! Thank You for drawing _____ out of the kingdom of darkness and into your light. According to the Word, I bind the Deaf and Dumb Spirit from the lives of the youth of our nation, and from our elderly. Father, I pray that You give them eyes to see and ears to hear what Your Spirit is saying. Even for those who sit in churches, but do not know You; Lord I pray that You will open their eyes that they may see You as You are. You said, without a vision the people perish. Lord the body of Messiah needs a vision of who you are! Open our eyes and ears Lord. You said without a vision the people perish. Open our ears Lord. You said that Your sheep hear Your voice and they follow You. We are the sheep of Your pasture. Thank You for being the Good Shepherd. Loosen the bonds of wickedness that others may come through the narrow gate, into Your fold, and be saved, Amen.

Declarations at the Gate of Simeon/ Deaf and Dumb Spirit

MATTHEW 15:10
"And after He called the multitude to him, He said to them, Hear, and understand."

JOHN 10:3
"To him the doorkeeper opens, and the sheep hear his voice, and he calls his own sheep by name, and leads them out."

JOHN 10:27
"My sheep hear My voice, and I know them, and they follow Me."

MATTHEW 11:15
"He who has ears to hear let him hear."

JOHN 5:24
"Truly, truly, I say to you, he who hears My word, and believes Him who sent Me, has eternal life, and does not come into judgment, but has passed out of death into life."

JAMES 1:19
"This you know, my beloved brethren, But let everyone be quick to hear, slow to speak, and slow to anger;"

ROMANS 10:17
"So faith comes from hearing and hearing by the word of Christ."

PROVERBS 20:12
"The hearing ear and the seeing eye, The Lord has made both of them."

HEBREWS 5:11
"Concerning him we have much to say, and it is hard to explain, since you have become dull of hearing."

PSALM 66:18
"If I regard wickedness in my heart, The Lord will not hear; But certainly God has heard; He has given heed to the voice of my prayer."

1st JOHN 5:14-15
"And this is the confidence which we have before Him, that, if we ask anything according to His will, He hears us. And if we know that He hears us in whatever we ask, we know that we have the requests which we have asked from Him."

MARK 8:18
"Having eyes do you not see? And having ears do you not hear? And do you not remember when I broke the five loaves, for the five thousand, how many baskets full of broken pieces you picked up? They said to Him, Twelve."

Praying at the Gate of Judah
Attacking Stronghold: Spirit of Perversion
Key: Holiness

Our God is an awesome God, Who reigns from heaven above – with wisdom, power and love! Lord I praise You. I cover myself today with the blood of Your Son. Thank You for forgiving all my iniquities. Thank You Yeshua that old things are passed away and all things have become new. I stand today before the gate of Judah and I bind perversion. I want to lift my voice and say, "I love You!" You mean everything to me and I will praise Your Name. Lord, You inhabit the praises of Your people. I want to rejoice and dance before You. I want you to fill me up today, Holy Spirit. Fall fresh on me. Melt me, mold me, fill me, use me Holy Spirit. Lord if there is rebellion or hate in my heart, then remove it from me as I begin to praise You. I confess those dark areas in my heart and I give You permission to heal the wounds and to bring light into those dark places.

Lord, I lift up _____ at the Gate of Judah, and I bind a spirit of perversion from operating in their life. Lord, set them free from wrong teaching, wrong thinking and from perverting the gospel. You came to set the captives free. I bind _____ to the truth and command a spirit of perversion to be silent. Perversion, and every associated manifestation may not operate in _____'s life or in their thoughts. I thank You that _____ will love the Lord their God with all their heart, all their strength, and their entire mind. God, I remind You that Your Word states that You will perfect everything that concerns _____. Teach them concerning Your ways, that they may walk in your paths. See to it that no one take _____ captive through philosophy and empty deception according to the tradition of men, rather than according to Messiah. Let them trust in the Lord with all of their heart, and not lean on their own understanding, in all their ways let _____ acknowledge You and You will make their paths straight.

Declarations at the Gate of Judah/ Spirit of Perversion

COLOSSIANS 2:8
"See to it that no one takes you captive through philosophy and empty deception, according to the tradition of men, according to the elementary principles of the world, rather than according to Christ."

LUKE 3:4-6
"The voice of one crying in the wilderness, Make ready the way of the LORD. Make his paths straight. Every ravine shall be filled up and every mountain and hill shall be brought low; and the crooked shall become straight, and the rough roads smooth; And all flesh shall see the salvation of GOD."

ISAIAH 2:3
"And many peoples will come and say, Come, let us go up to the mountain of the Lord, to the house of the God of Jacob. That He may teach us concerning his ways, and that we may walk in His paths."

PSALM 1:1
"How blessed is the man who does not walk in the counsel of the wicked, nor stand in the path of sinners, nor sit in the seat of scoffers! But his delight is in the law of the LORD and in his law he meditates day and night."

PSALM 119:105
"Thy word is a lamp to my feet and a light to my path."

PSALM 139:23-24
"Search me, O God, and know my heart; Try me and know my anxious thoughts; And see if there be any hurtful way in me And lead me in the everlasting way."

PROV 3:5-6
"Trust in the Lord with all of your heart, And do not lean on your own understanding. In all your ways acknowledge Him and He will make your paths straight."

1st CORINTHIANS 6:13
"...Yet the body is not meant for immorality but for the Lord and the Lord for the body."

1st CORINTHIANS 6:18-20
"Flee immorality. Every other sin that a man commits is outside his body, but the immoral man sins against his own body. For you have been bought with a price: therefore glorify God in your body."

PSALM 19:12
"Who can discern his errors? Acquit me of hidden faults."

DEUTERONOMY 23:14
"Since the LORD your God walks in the midst of your camp to deliver you and to defeat your enemies before you, therefore

*your camp must be holy; and He must not
see anything indecent among you lest he turn
away from you."*

EZEKIEL 36:25-27
*"Then I will sprinkle clean water on you,
and you will be clean; I will cleanse you
from all of your filthiness and from all of
your idols. Moreover, I will give you a new
heart and put a new spirit within you; and I
will remove the heart of stone from your flesh
and give you a heart of flesh. And I will put
My Spirit within you and I will cause you to
walk in My statutes and you will be careful to
observe My ordinances."*

Praying at the Gate of Zebulon
Attacking Stronghold: Familiar Spirits
Key: Repentance

Lord, I cover myself, my family, my future, and my
finances with the blood of Jesus. I thank You for protection
and wisdom. Hide me Lord in the cleft of the rock. Holy
Spirit, teach me how to pray at this Gate of Zebulon. Reveal
to me what is on the Father's heart and make me in sync
with His heart. It is wise to speak to the enemy at the gate,
therefore I come before you at the Gate of Zebulon and I
bind all familiar spirits that would attempt to inhabit your
rightful place in _____'s heart. Lord you said, Be
thou holy for I am holy. I desire to walk in Your holiness. If
there is anything in my house that is not pleasing to You or
that has a curse attached to it; please reveal it that I may
remove it. Cleanse me – spirit, soul and body. I am Your
temple. Father, I lift up my children and my grandchildren

to you, and I bind all familiar spirits that would want to oppress and seduce these little ones through video games, books, music, magazine, television, movies, the internet, computers, board games and jewelry. Father, I pray that my children, my grandchildren and _____ would have a hunger and a thirst after righteousness. Establish our footsteps in Your Word and let no iniquity have dominion over us. I bind our minds to the mind of Messiah and our will to the will of the Father. I loose and destroy wrong patterns of thinking, wrong ideas and wrong attitudes that may be in our minds. Father, I build a hedge of protection around us with words of life and truth. I believe that we will know You and love You with all of our hearts, minds and strength. Lord, I ask You to forgive those in my ancestral line who went after foreign gods and served them. I place the cross of Yeshua and the blood of Yeshua between myself and those in my past generations who walked away from You in their hearts. You became a curse for us Yeshua and I thank You that from here on, the seed of the righteous will be blessed of God. Create in us a clean heart O God, and renew a right spirit within us. Cast us not away from Your presence. Don't take Your Holy Spirit from us. Then we will teach transgressors Your ways and sinners shall be converted unto Thee. Bring us in through the Gate of Zebulon that we may behold your beauty in the Holy of Holies. We come to You through the blood of the Lamb. You are our righteousness and sanctification and we thank You, Lord. Amen.

Declarations at the Gate of Zebulon/Familiar Spirits

ISAIAH 1:16
"Wash yourselves, make yourselves clean;
Remove the evil of your deeds from My sight.
Cease to do evil."

ISAIAH 1:4
"Alas, sinful nation. People weighed down with iniquity, Offspring of evildoers, Sons who act corruptly. They have abandoned the LORD. They have despised the Holy One of Israel. They have turned away from Him. Where will you be stricken again, As you continue in your rebellion?"

DEUTERONOMY 18:9
"When you enter the land which the LORD your God gives you, you shall not learn to imitate the detestable things of those nations..."

DEUTERONOMY 7:26
"And you shall not bring an abomination into your house, and like it come under the ban (curse); you shall utterly detest it and you shall utterly abhor it, for it is something banned."

1st PETER 2:16
"Act as free men, and do not use your freedom as a covering for evil, but use it as bond slaves of God."

ROMANS 6:22
"But now having been freed from sin and enslaved to God, you derive your benefit, resulting in sanctification, and the outcome, eternal life."

REVELATION 21:8
"But the cowardly and unbelieving and

abominable and murderers and immoral persons and sorcerers and idolaters and all liars, their part will be in the lake that burns with fire and brim-stone, which is the second death."

MATTHEW 12:43-45

"Now when the unclean spirit goes out of a man, it passes through waterless places, seeking rest, and does not find it. Then it says, 'I will return to my house from which I came', and when it comes, it finds it unoccupied, swept, and put in order. Then it goes, and takes along with it seven other spirits more wicked than itself, and they go in and they live there; and the last state of that man becomes worse than the first. This is the way it will also be with this evil generation."

Praying at the Gate of Levi
Attacking Spirit: Lying Spirit
Key: The Word

Abba, I come before You today and ask You to cover me with the blood of Yeshua. Hide me under the shadow of Your wings. Lord, I know that You have given me authority over the enemy and that nothing will harm me. I want to stand in the gap for my congregation. I can't take the speck out of my brother's eye before I take the log out of my own eye. Lord, if I have any manifestations of a Lying Spirit at work within me, I ask that You would reveal it and cleanse me from all hidden sins. I stand before the Gate of Levi and I bind a lying spirit, and all the associated manifestations, especially a religious spirit. I pray that this religious spirit and lying stronghold will not be able to operate in any way in my church, my fellowship group, my family or my own life. The blood of Yeshua is against you, Lying Spirit! Father I bind _____ to the truth of the word. I also bind the Jewish people to the truth of the gospel. Jesus, You said, "I am the Way, the Truth and the Life – no one comes to the Father but through You." I declare and decree this at the Gate of Levi.

Yeshua, You came to set the captives free and to mend the brokenhearted. I lift up _____ to you, and I bring them before the Gate of Levi. Lord, if they are walking in a homosexual lifestyle, I ask you to cut them free from that Lying Spirit. Bring them through the Gate of Levi into Your presence. Reveal the truth to them and free them from all deception or lies that they may have believed. Loosen the bonds of wickedness in their lives. Lord, You said that You came for the sick, not for the healthy. _____ cannot set himself/herself free. I pray that You be glorified through their life and make their life a testimony of your power in Yeshua Name.

Thank You, Lord that there is no condemnation to them that are in Messiah Jesus, Lord even when we sin, thank You that we have an Advocate with the Father. Thank You for Your blood, which cleanses me of guilt, sin, shame and failure. Thank You that You remove my sin from me as far as the east is from the west. If I abide in You and Your Words abide in me, I will know the truth and the truth will set me free. I bind myself to the truth. Thank You for being my Deliverer. Your Word is truth. Help me, Holy Spirit to hide Your Word in my heart that I might not sin against You. Amen.

Support Scriptures at the Gate of Levi/Lying Spirit

ZECHARIAH 8:16
'These are the things which you should do:

speak the truth to one another; judge with truth and judgments for peace in your gates."

ZECHARIAH 8:3
"Thus says the LORD, I will return to Zion and will dwell in the midst of Jerusalem. Then Jerusalem will be called the City of Truth, and the mountain of the LORD of Hosts will be called the Holy Mountain."

PROVERBS 12:17
"He who speaks truth tells what is right, But a false witness deceit."

PROVERBS 3:3-4
"Do not let kindness and truth leave you; Bind them around your neck, Write them on the tablet of your heart. So you will find favor and good repute in the sight of God and man."

ROMANS 3:4
"May it never be! Rather, let God be found true, though every man be found a liar,"

JOHN 8:31-32
"If you abide in My word, then you are truly disciples of Mine; and you shall know the truth, and the truth shall make you free."

JOHN 14:6
"I am the way, and the truth, and the life; no one comes to the Father but through Me."

ROMANS 1:25
"For they exchanged the truth of God for a lie, and worshipped and served the creature rather than the Creator who is blessed forever. Amen."

PROVERBS 19:5
"A false witness will not go unpunished, And he who tells lies will not escape."

COLOSSIANS 3: 9-10
"Do not lie to one another, since you laid aside the old self, with its evil practices and have put on the new self who is being renewed to a true knowledge according to the image of the One who created him"

COLOSSIANS 2:8
"See to it that no one takes you captive through philosophy and empty deception, according to the tradition of men, according to the elementary principles of the world, rather than according to Christ."

REVELATION 21:8
"But for the cowardly and unbelieving and abominable and murderers and immoral persons and sorcerers and idolaters and all liars, their part will be in the lake that burns with fire and brimstone, which is the second death."

Praying at the Gate of Issachar
Attacking Stronghold: Spirit of Whoredom
Key: Giving

Yeshua, I bless You and thank You for Your blood. You are my Refuge and my Fortress, my God in Whom I trust. You will deliver me and _____ from the snare of the trapper and from the deadly pestilence. No evil will befall us. No plague will come near our dwelling place. I thank You for giving Your angels charge over us in all our ways. I speak the blood of Yeshua over myself, and _____ and over our households, our futures, our finances and everything that concerns us. Holy Spirit, come and teach us how to pray through this Gate of Issachar. We acknowledge Your presence and our dependence on You. Show us what is on the Father's heart to pray at this gate. Lord, we stand before this gate and ask You to search our hearts and to see if there are any manifestations of this stronghold hiding in us. Your Word says that they overcame the enemy by the blood of the Lamb and the word of their testimonies and that they loved not their own lives even unto the death. Father, I bind a Spirit of Whoredom in our lives. All associations and manifestations like the love of money, the love of the world, or idolatry, I ask You to command deliverance for me and _____. Acquit us of secret sins. Lord, Your Word says to love the Lord your God with all of your heart, your strength and your might. I ask You to cause me and _____ to love You with our whole hearts. I pray that _____ and I would obey your commands. Write Your law upon our hearts O Lord, and cause us to walk in obedience. You desire obedience more than sacrifice. Help us to seek first Your kingdom and Your righteousness and all these things shall be added unto us. I know that if _____ or I delight ourselves in You, then You will give us the desires of our hearts.

Father, it is Your will to set the captives free. To loosen the bonds of wickedness, to undo the bands of the yoke. Lord if _____ is bound by pornography, fornication, homosexuality, adultery, prostitution or any such evil, I know it is not your will that they would be bound by these things. Lord, as I bring _____ before the Gate of Issachar, I bind the Spirit of Whoredom. I speak the blood of Yeshua against you. I bind the unclean spirit and any of its manifestations in _____'s life. Lord, establish _____'s footsteps in Your Word and let no iniquity have dominion over _____. Mend _____'s heart and heal _____ of all their wounds. Amen.

Declarations at the Gate of Issachar/ Spirit of Whoredom

1st JOHN 2:15-16
"Do not love the world nor the things in the world. If anyone loves the world, the love of the Father is not in him. For all that is in the world, the lust of the flesh and the lust of the eyes, and the boastful pride of life, is not from the Father, but is from the world."

1st THESSALONIANS 4:3-5
"For this is the will of God, your sanctification; that is, that you abstain from sexual immorality; that each of you know how to posses his own vessel in sanctification and honor, not in lustful passion, like the Gentiles who do not know God."

1st CORINTHIANS 6: 16-20
"Or do you not know that the one who joins himself to a harlot is one body with her? For

He says, The two will become one flesh. But the one who joins himself to the Lord is one spirit with Him. Flee immorality. Every other sin that a man commits is outside the body, but the immoral man sins against his own body. Or do you not know that your body is a temple of the Holy Spirit who is in you, whom you have from God, and that you are not your own? For you have been bought with a price therefore glorify God in your body."

COLOSSIANS 3:5
"Therefore consider the members of your earthly body as dead to immorality, impurity, passion, evil desire, and greed, which amounts to idolatry."

1st CORINTHIANS 10:7-8
"And do not be idolaters, as some of them were; Nor let us act immorally, as some of them did and twenty-three thousand fell in one day."

ROMANS 12:1-2
"I urge you therefore, brethren, by the mercies of God, to present your bodies a living and holy sacrifice, acceptable to God, which is your spiritual service of worship. And do not be conformed to this world, but be transformed by the renewing of your mind, that you may prove what the will of God is, that which is good and acceptable and perfect."

ISAIAH 35:8
*"And a highway will be there, a roadway.
And it will be called the Highway of
Holiness. The unclean will not travel on it,
But it will be for him who walks that way,
And fools will not wander on it."*

Praying at the Gate of Benjamin
Attacking Stronghold: Spirit of Pride
Key: Humility

Abba, as I come before You today to intercede for my family, my church, this nation, and the nation of _____, I need Your wisdom in how to pray. Father, I know you said, that if my people, which are called by My name, will humble themselves, pray, and seek Your face and turn from their wicked ways, You will hear from heaven, forgive our sins and heal our land. Search my heart God, and see if there be any hurtful way in me and lead me in the way everlasting. I confess areas of stubbornness, self-righteousness, arrogance and/or pride on my own heart. As I ponder the manifestations of a Spirit of Pride, reveal to me truth in my inward parts. God, as I come before You, acknowledging my sins, set me free so that I might serve You with a willing spirit. At the Gate of Benjamin, I bind according to Your Word, a Spirit of Pride in my own life. As I make these declarations at this gate with authority, I ask You to watch over Your Word to perform it. Your Word goes forth and does not return empty or void. It accomplishes what it was sent forth to do. Create in me a clean heart, and renew a right spirit within me. Cast me not away from Your presence and take not Your Holy Spirit from me. Then I will teach transgressors Your ways and sinners will be converted unto Thee.

Lord, I lift up _____ to you. I take authority over the stronghold of Pride and every associated manifestation in _____'s life. Cause _____ to walk in a manner worthy of Your calling. Let _____ walk in the fear of the Lord, which is to hate evil, pride, arrogance and the evil way. Lord, establish _____'s footsteps in Your Word and let no iniquity have dominion over _____.

I pray that this nation will never forget that it is You; God Who gives us the power to make wealth. Riches and honor come from You alone. Help us as a people to turn from our wicked ways and to do justice, love kindness and to walk humbly with our God. We pray for our President and for all those who are in authority over us, that they would humble themselves before You and seek wisdom from above. I pray that they commit their plans to You. Thank You for establishing their thoughts. You resist the proud but give grace to the humble. Help us, Holy One of Israel to walk in humility. Amen

Support Scriptures at the Gate of Benjamin/ Spirit of Pride

MICAH 6:8
"...and what does the Lord require of you But to do justice, to love kindness, and to walk humbly with your God"

2nd CHRONICLES 34:27
"Because your heart was tender and you humbled yourself before God, when you heard His words against this place and against it's inhabitants, and because you humbled yourself before Me, tore your clothes, and wept before Me, I truly have heard you," declares the LORD."

JOEL 2:13a
"...And rend your hearts and not your garments."

2nd CHRONICLES 7:14
"...and my people who are called by my name humble themselves and pray, and seek my face, and turn from their wicked ways, then I will hear from heaven, will forgive their sin, and will heal their land."

JAMES 4:6
"But He gives a greater grace. Therefore it says, God is opposed to the proud, but gives grace to the humble."

JAMES 4:10
"Humble yourselves in the presence of the Lord and He will exalt you."

1st PETER 5:6
"Humble yourselves, therefore, under the mighty hand of God, that He may exalt you at the proper time."

PROVERBS 16:18
"Pride goes before destruction, and a haughty spirit before stumbling."

PROVERBS 8:13
"The fear of the LORD is to hate evil; pride and arrogance and the evil way, and the perverted mouth, I hate."

PROVERBS 18:12
"Before destruction the heart of a man is haughty, But humility goes before honor."

PROVERBS 22:4
"The reward of humility and the fear of the LORD are riches, honor and life."

Praying at the Gate of Naphtali
Attacking Stronghold: Spirit of Jealousy
Key: Love

Father, I come before You today, and I ask You to give _____ and me wisdom in how to go through this gate. First, I ask You to hide us in the cleft of the rock, under the shadow of Your wings. Thank You for the protection of the blood of Yeshua. You told us that if we confess our sins, You are faithful and just to forgive us our sins and cleanse us from all unrighteousness. I confess to You sins of anger, cruelty and selfishness. I ask You to change my and _____ 's heart. We know that we can do all things through Messiah who gives us strength. I bind jealousy from operating in my life as well as _____'s life. At the Gate of Naphtali, I ask You to give me the grace to be quick to hear, slow to anger and slow to speak. Lord, out of the abundance of the heart, the mouth speaks. I ask You to fill me and _____ today with Your love and kindness. The heart of the righteous ponders how to answer, but the mouth of the wicked pours out wicked things. Let me and _____ ponder how to answer today. I ask You for great understanding today. A person who is slow to anger has great understanding. Only through Your love and grace will ___ and I be able to walk in a manner worthy of Your calling.

You watch over Your Word to perform it. I declare at

this gate that _____ is patient and kind. _____ is not jealous. They do not brag. They are not arrogant. They do not act unbecomingly or seek their own way. _____ is not provoked. They do not take into account a wrong suffered. They do not rejoice with unrighteousness, but with the truth; they bear all things, believe all things and endure all things. _____ never fails.

Lord, I want to lift up my church to You today. I bind the Spirit of Jealousy from touching the worship team, the children's ministries, and every ministry and fellowship group in our congregation. Division and every associated manifestation are bound from operation in our midst. I pray for the pastoral and the administrative staff – that a spirit of harmony and peace would be released. Let each member of the staff walk in humility and gentleness, with patience, showing forbearance to one another in love being diligent to preserve the unity of the spirit in the bond of peace. I also want to pray for _____'s marriage, that jealousy, selfishness and suspicion would have no place in the minds' and hearts of _____ and _____. Lord, You said, How blessed it is for brethren to dwell together in unity. Amen and amen!

Supporting Scripture at the Gate of Naphtali/ Spirit of Jealousy

EPHESIANS 4:1-3
"I, Therefore, the prisoner of the Lord, entreat you to walk in a manner worthy of the calling, with which you have been called, with all humility and gentleness, with patience, showing forbearance to one another in love, being diligent to preserve the unity of the Spirit in the bond of peace."

PHILIPPIANS 2:3-4

"Do nothing from selfishness or empty conceit, but with humility of mind let each of you regard one another as more important than himself; do not merely look out for your own personal interests but also for the interests of others."

PHILIPPIANS 4:11-13

"Not that I speak from want; for I have learned to be content in whatever circumstances I am. I know how to get along with humble means, and I also know how to live in prosperity; in every and any circumstance I have learned the secret of being filled and going hungry, both of having abundance and suffering need. I can do all things through Him who strengthens me."

PROVERBS 22:24-25

"Do not associate with a man given to anger; or go with a hot-tempered man, lest you learn his ways, and find a snare for yourself."

PROVERBS 15:18

"A hot-tempered man stirs up strife, but the slow to anger pacifies contention."

PROVERBS 15:28

"The heart of the righteous ponders how to answer, but the mouth of the wicked pours out wicked things."

PROVERBS 15:1
"A gentle answer turns away wrath, but a harsh word stirs up anger."

PROVERBS 14:29
"He who is slow to anger has great understanding, But he who is quick-tempered exalts folly."

EPHESIANS 4:26
"Be angry, and yet do not sin. Do not let the sun go down on your anger and do not give the devil an opportunity."

EPHESIANS 4:31-32
"Let all bitterness, and wrath and anger and clamor and slander be put away from you, along with all malice and be kind to one another, tenderhearted, forgiving each other, just as God in Christ has forgiven you."

PSALM 145:8
"The Lord is gracious and merciful; Slow to anger and great in loving-kindness."

1ˢᵗ CORINTHIANS 13:4-8a
"Love is patient, love is kind, and is not jealous, love does not brag and is not arrogant, does not act unbecomingly, it does not seek its own, is not provoked, does not take into account a wrong suffered, does not rejoice with unrighteousness but rejoices with the truth; bears all things, believes all things, hopes all things, and endures all things, love never fails."

Praying at the Gate of Gad
Attacking Stronghold: Spirit of Fear
Key: Faith

Father, I come before You today, just to praise You and thank You for the blood of Yeshua. I speak that blood over everything that concerns me. I thank You Father that no weapon formed against me can prosper. You said in Your Word, that it is wise to speak to the enemy at the gate. Right now, I come before the Gate of Gad. You have given me keys to the kingdom and said, "Whatever I bind on earth will be bound in heaven and whatever I loose on earth will be loosed in heaven." Father, with these keys, I bind a Spirit of Fear from operating in _____'s life. LORD, You did not give _____ a spirit of fear, but of love, power and a sound mind. You said, "Be anxious for nothing, but with prayer, supplication and thanksgiving, let your requests be made known to God, and the peace of God which passes all under-standing will guard your hearts and minds in Yeshua Ha Mashiach. Thank You, Lord, that You are Jehovah Shalom my and _____'s peace. Father, it is Your will that _____ and I prosper and be in health even as our souls prosper. I thank You that everything I or _____ touch today will be blessed. Command Your blessing upon us that we will be blessed as we come in and as we go out. Greater is He who is in us than he who is in the world. Yeshua, we know that we can do all things through You, because You give us strength. Thank You that You fight our battles, Lord. You are our light and our salvation, whom shall we fear? You are the defense of our lives, of whom shall we be afraid? Even when the enemies come in to devour our flesh, they will stumble and fall. Though a host encamps against us, our hearts will not fear. Though war rise up against us, we will not be afraid. You will hide us in Your secret place. We bless Your Name. Lord, in Your Name, we bind every associated manifestation of a Spirit of Fear in our lives. Lord, we cast our cares upon You because You care for us.

Lord, You said that perfect love casts out fear and the torment that comes with fear. I thank You that You have told us, "Fear not!" Thank You for Your love and mercy. We put our trust in You. Amen

Declarations at the Gate of Gad/Spirit of Fear

2nd TIMOTHY 1:7
"For God has not given us a spirit of timidity, but of power, and love, and discipline."

PSALM 34:4
"I sought the LORD, and He answered me. And delivered me from all of my fears."

PSALM 34:7
"The angel of the Lord encamps around those who fear Him, and rescues them."

PSALM 27:1-3
"The LORD is my light and my salvation; Whom shall I fear? The LORD is the defense of my life; Whom shall I dread? Though a host encamp against me, My heart will not fear, Though war arise against me, in spite of this I shall be confident."

PSALM 27:13
"I would have despaired unless I had believed that I would see the goodness of the LORD in the land of the living."

PSALM 56:3-4
"When I am afraid, I will put my trust is Thee. In God, whose word I praise, In God I have put my trust; I shall not be afraid."

PSALM 60:12
"Through God we shall do valiantly, And it is He who will tread down our adversaries."

PSALM 37:25
"I have been young, and now I am old; Yet I have not seen the righteous forsaken, or His descendants begging bread."

PSALM 23:4
"Even though I walk through the valley of the shadow of death, I fear no evil; for Thou art with me. Thy rod and Thy staff, they comfort me."

JOHN 14:27b
"Let not your heart be troubled, nor let it be fearful."

MATTHEW 6:34
"Therefore do not be anxious for tomorrow; for tomorrow will care for itself. Each day has enough trouble of its own."

PHILIPPIANS 4:6-7
"Be anxious for nothing, but in everything by prayer and supplication with thanksgiving let your requests be made known to God. And the peace of God which surpasses all comprehension shall guard your hearts and

your minds in Christ Jesus."

Praying at the Gate of Joseph
Attacking Stronghold: Spirit of Infirmity
Key: Worship

Father, thank You that You purchased me with the blood of Your spotless Lamb, Yeshua. I thank You that the life of the flesh is in the blood. I speak the blood over me, around me, between evil and me and between me and the author of all evil. Holy Spirit, teach me how to pray through this gate, and reveal to me those who need a touch in their physical bodies as well as their emotions. I welcome You, Holy Spirit. Father, You said, "I am the Lord your Healer." Glory to Your Name. Thank You for remembering Your covenant of healing. You have given me the keys of the kingdom, and in the Name of Yeshua, I take authority over the Spirit of Infirmity at the Gate of Joseph and I bind it according to Your Word. Lord, You say in Your Word, that if I regard iniquity in my heart, You will not hear me. Search my heart, O Lord. Father, I confess all known sin to You and I thank You that Your blood covers me. Lord it is Your will that _____ or I be made whole. The blood of Yeshua is against you, you Spirit of Infirmity. You have no legal right or access to me or to _____. The blood of Yeshua has the power to cleanse me even from the effect that sin has had in my life. If _____ or I are not wise in our own eyes, and turn from evil, this will bring health to our bodies and nourishment to our bones. Help us to turn from evil, Lord. Bless the Lord, O my soul, and all that is within _____, or me bless His holy Name. Bless the Lord, Who pardons all of my or _____'s iniquities and heals all of our diseases. Lord, I lift up not only those who have physical needs, but those who are hurting emotionally. Holy Spirit, comfort _____. You are the One Who comes alongside and comes to the aid of the hurting. Reveal Yourself to _____. Lord, send your ministering angels to perform Your will. I know You came to give life and give it more abundantly. Allow the river of life to flow through _____'s spirit, bringing healing, wholeness, resurrection power and restoration. I remind You Lord, that You said, "Many are the afflictions of the righteous, but He delivers them out of them all." If I lay hands on the sick, they will recover. Lord, I pray that I, my family, my Pastor, the members of my church, my employees and _____ would dwell in the secret place of the Most High. Thank You for your divine protection and for giving your angels charge over_____ and me. Thank You Lord that no evil will befall _____ or will any plague come nigh ____'s dwelling. In Jesus' Name, Amen.

Support Scriptures at the Gate of Joseph/ Spirit of Infirmity

JEREMIAH 17:14
> *"Heal me, O Lord, and I will be healed; Save me and I will be saved. For Thou art my praise."*

EXODUS 15:26
> *"And He said, If you will give earnest heed to the voice of the LORD your God, and do what is right in His sight, and give ear to His commandments, and keep all His statutes, I will put none of the diseases on you which I have put on the Egyptians, for I, the LORD am your healer."*

DEUTERONOMY 7:15
> *"And the Lord will remove from you all*

sickness; and He will not put on you any of the harmful diseases of Egypt which you have known, but He will lay them on all who hate you."

EXODUS 23:25
"But you shall serve the LORD your God, and He will bless your bread and your water; and I will remove sickness from your midst."

PROVERBS 3:7-8
"Do not be wise in your own eyes; Fear the LORD and turn away from evil. It will be healing to your body, and refreshment to your bones."

PROVERBS 4:20-22
"My son, give attention to my words; Incline your ear to my sayings. Do not let them depart from your sight; Keep them in the midst of your heart. For they are life to those who find them, and health to all their whole body."

PSALM 103:1-5
"Bless the LORD, O my soul; And all that is within me, bless His holy name. Bless the LORD, O my soul and forget none of His benefits. Who pardons all of your iniquities; Who heals all your diseases; Who redeems your life from the pit; who crowns you with lovingkindness and compassion; Who satisfies your years with good things so that your youth is renewed like the eagle."

3rd JOHN vs.2
"Beloved, I pray that in all respects you may prosper and be in good health, just as your soul prospers."

ACTS 10:38
"You know of Jesus of Nazareth, how God anointed Him with the Holy Spirit, and with power, and how He went about doing good, and healing all who were oppressed by the devil, for God was with Him."

MATTHEW 8:16-17
"And when evening had come, they brought to Him many who were demon-possessed; and He cast out the spirits with a word, and healed all who were ill in order that what was spoken through Isaiah the prophet might be fulfilled, saying, He Himself took our infirmities and carried away our diseases."

MATTHEW 9:35
"And Jesus was going about all the cities and the villages, teaching in their synagogues and proclaiming the gospel of the kingdom, and healing every kind of disease and every kind of sickness."

MARK 16:17-18
"And these signs will accompany those who have believed: in My name they will cast out demons, they will speak with new tongues; they will pick up serpents, and if they drink any deadly poison, it shall not hurt them; they will lay hands on the sick, and they will recover."

Praying at the Gate of Asher
Attacking Stronghold: Spirit of Heaviness
Key: Praise

Lord, I come before You at the Gate of Asher. I know that You have given me power over the enemy and nothing by any means can harm me. I bind my mind this day to the mind of Messiah, and I bind my will to the will of the Father. The blood of Yeshua has purchased my household and me. Lord, no weapon formed against me can prosper. Holy Spirit, I ask you to come and help me go through the Gate of Asher into Your presence where there is fullness of joy. Lord, You alone are worthy to be praised! I will enter Your gates with thanksgiving and Your courts with praise. Thank You Yeshua for the oil of gladness, instead of mourning. I receive it by faith. Thank You for the mantle of praise instead of a spirit of heaviness. You said, "The ransomed of the Lord will return and come with joyful shouting unto Zion, with everlasting joy upon their heads. They will find gladness and joy and sorrow and sighing will flea away. Lord I know that You watch over Your Word to perform it; and that Your Word goes out and does not return empty or void – without accomplishing all that You send it out to do. All sorrow, sadness and hopelessness must flee in the Name of Jesus. Your Word says that I would have despaired unless I had believed that I would see the goodness of the Lord in the land of the living. Thank You God that regardless of the circumstances I find myself in, I believe that I will see Your goodness in the land of the living. I know that You work all things together for my good. Arise O Lord, and let my enemies be scattered! I bind every manifestation of the spirit of heaviness from operating in my life today. The blood of Yeshua is against you, you Spirit of Heaviness. You are bound from operating in my life, in the lives of my family, in the lives of my Pastors, my church and all those whom

God brings before me. I praise You, Jesus. I offer You the sacrifice of praise. I will bless You at all times; your praise shall continually be in my mouth. You are the glory and the lifter of my head. Your joy is my strength and in Your presence there is fullness of joy. I want to come before You now with singing. Shouts of joy and victory resound in the tents of the righteous of the Lord! The Lord's right hand has done mighty things for us; the Lord's right hand is lifted high! Thank You God that You have turned my mourning into dancing. I praise you in Jesus' Name, Amen.

Declarations at the Gate of Asher/Spirit of Heaviness

ISAIAH 61:3a
"To grant those who mourn in Zion, giving them a garland instead of ashes, The oil of gladness instead of mourning. The mantle of praise instead of a spirit of fainting."

ISAIAH 35:10
"And the ransomed of the LORD will return, and come with joyful shouting unto Zion, with everlasting joy upon their heads. They will find gladness and joy, and sorrow and sighing will flee away."

PSALM 118:15
"The sound of joyful shouting and salvation is in the tents of the righteous; The right hand of the LORD does valiantly."

PSALM 97:12
"Be glad in the LORD, you righteous ones; And give thanks to His holy name."

PSALM 33:21
"For our heart rejoices in Him, Because we trust in His holy name."

ISAIAH 55:12
"For you will go out with joy, and be led forth with peace, The mountains and the hills will break forth into shouts of joy before you, and all the trees of the field will clap their hands."

PSALM 68:3
"But let the righteous be glad; let them exult before God; Yes let them rejoice with gladness."

PSALM 30:11a
"Thou hast turned for me my mourning into dancing;"

EPHESIANS 5:18-19
"And do not get drunk with wine, for that is dissipation, but be filled with the Spirit, speaking to one another in psalms, and hymns and spiritual songs, singing and making melody with your heart to the Lord."

ROMANS 14:17
"...for the kingdom of God is not eating and drinking, but righteousness, and peace, and joy in the Holy Spirit."

NEHEMIAH 8:10b
"Do not be grieved for the joy of the LORD is your strength."

PHILIPPIANS 4:4
"Rejoice in the LORD always, again I will say, rejoice!"

Praying at the Gate of Dan
Attacking Stronghold: Bondage
Key: Holy Spirit

Father, I come before You today and I worship You. You are the Lord of lords and the King of kings. I know You are a righteous Judge. I thank You that You sent Yeshua into the world to save _____ and not to condemn _____. Right now Lord, I apply the blood of Yeshua to _____'s life and to their family. I thank You that You said You would be a wall of fire around _____ and that Your glory would be in _____'s midst. Father, search my heart. If there is any unforgiveness, reveal it to me that I may confess, repent and be cleansed of all unrighteousness. I confess that I have had difficulty coming before You in prayer. As I come before the Gate of Dan, I declare that You are a righteous Judge and I bind bondage from operating in my life and in the life of _____ this very day. Jesus, You came to mend the brokenhearted and to set the captives free. You told me that if I abide in You and Your Word abides in me, that I would know the truth and the truth would set me free. Thank You Lord for liberty. Help me and help _____ to walk in a manner worthy of Your calling. Lord, Your anointing is what breaks the yoke of bondage. Your yoke is easy and Your burden is light. I want to be yoked with you. Let Your anointing and Your presence rest on _____ and me. Lord, I lift up to You those who are in prison and I bind a spirit of bondage in their lives. Thank You that You are my and _____ 's Deliverer. You are our stronghold. You are our very present help in times of trouble. You are a refuge for the oppressed. You said that You would never leave us or forsake us. Father, You know the areas where _____ and I have yielded to sin. I confess the idolatry in my life by trying to satisfy my soul with compulsive behaviors. I know that you came for those who are sick and not healthy. I come to ask for Your help in time of need. Deliver me and _____ from (addictive behaviors). I ask You to forgive me from judging others. If I judge, it will be measured back to me, so I release myself from that judgment now, and I repent. I would ask You, Lord to forgive the sins of my fore-fathers in how they sinned against You to the fourth genera-tion. I remind You, Lord that You said if a thief were found out, he has to restore 7 times what he has stolen. Also Lord, Your covenant states that if I tithe, You will rebuke the devourer on my behalf. Thank You Lord for Your righteous judgments. Lord, thank You that Your mercy triumphs over judgment. In Jesus' Name, Amen.

Declarations at the Gate of Dan/Spirit of Bondage

2nd CORINTHIANS 4:3-4
"And even if our gospel is veiled, it is veiled to those who are perishing, in whose case the god of this world has blinded the minds of the unbelieving, that they might not see the light of the gospel of the glory of Christ, who is the image of God."

MATTHEW 6:12; 14-15
"And forgive us our debts as we have also forgiven our debtors. For if you forgive men for their transgressions, your heavenly Father will also forgive you: But if you do not forgive men, then your Father will not forgive your transgressions."

MARK 11:24-25
"Therefore I say to you, all things for which you pray and ask, believe that you have received them, and they shall be granted you. And whenever you stand praying, forgive, if you have anything against anyone; so that your Father also who is in heaven may forgive you your transgressions. But if you do not forgive neither will your Father who is in heaven forgive your transgressions."

PSALM 66:18
"If I regard wickedness in my heart, The Lord will not hear."

ISAIAH 61:1
"The Spirit of the Lord GOD is upon me, Because the LORD has anointed me, To bring good news to the afflicted; He has sent me to bind up the brokenhearted, To proclaim liberty to captives, and freedom to prisoners."

ROMANS 6:10-12
"For the death that He died, He died to sin, once for all; but the life that He lives, He lives to God. Even so consider yourselves to be dead to sin, but alive to God in Christ Jesus. Therefore do not let sin reign in your mortal body that you should obey its lusts."

PSALM 119-133
"Establish my footsteps in Thy word and do not let any iniquity have dominion over me."

PSALM 119:11
"Thy word I have treasured in my heart, that I may not sin against Thee."

EPHESIANS 5:18-19
"And do not get drunk with wine for that is dissipation, but be filled with the Spirit, speaking to one another with psalms and hymns, and spiritual songs, singing and making melody with your heart to the Lord."

1st PETER 4:1
"Therefore, since Christ has suffered in the flesh, arm yourselves also with the same purpose, because he who has suffered in the flesh has ceased from sin."

CHAPTER 12

Entering Through the Narrow Gate

※※

Whether you are a Jew or a Gentile, you may find yourself wondering, "Just what does it mean to be born again?"

> *"And now, if you diligently obey my voice, and shall guard my covenant, then you shall be my treasured possessions above all the peoples; for all the earth is mine."* (Shemoth/ Exodus 19:5)

This word wasn't given just to Judah but to the whole house of Yisrael. When the Jews left Egypt, a mixed multitude of people came out among them. Those who were not born Yisraelites became one with them by joining themselves to the Yisraelites and accepting the covenant with YHVH (God). *"And a mixed multitude went up with them too, also flocks and herds, very much livestock."* (Shemoth/Exodus 12:38)

When YHVH (God) created Adam, He created him in

absolute perfection — without sin. From Adam, God created Eve, and gave them free will. God created MAN to be in perfect, face-to-face, communication with Him; however, Adam and Eve (of their own free will) chose to listen to the serpent. When they made that choice, they disobeyed YHVH's commandment not to eat of the tree of the knowledge of good and evil, thus separating themselves from YHVH.

> *"And the serpent said to the woman, You shall certainly not die. For Elohim (God) knows that in the day you eat of it your eyes shall be opened, and you shall be like Elohim (God), knowing good from evil. And the woman saw that the tree was good for food, that it was pleasant to the eyes, and a tree desirable to make one wise, and she took of its fruit and ate. And she also gave to her husband with her, and he ate."* (Bereshith/Genesis 3:4-6)

Sin entered YHVH's perfect creation. From Adam, sin has been passed down through all generations. *"For this reason, even as through ONE man sin did enter the world, and death through sin, and thus death spread to all men, because ALL sinned."* (Romans 5:12)

From Adam to this very time, man has walked in his own understanding, wisdom, and philosophies — not recognizing or acknowledging his failure to walk in YHVH's wisdom, principles, and commandments. This is true of both Jew and Gentile.

> *"Trust in YHVH with ALL your heart AND lean not on YOUR OWN understanding; Know HIM in ALL your ways, and HE makes ALL your paths straight. Do not be wise in*

your own eyes, Fear YHVH and Turn
(Repent) away from evil. It is healing to your
navel, and moistening to your bones."
(Mishle/Proverbs 3:5-8)

YHVH made provision, for our atonement, our redemption, and our salvation and for ALL our sin, through the shed BLOOD of perfect, flawless, sacrificial animals.

"Let the lamb be a perfect one, a year old
male. Take it from the sheep or from the
goats... vs 7. and they shall take some of the
blood and put it on the doorposts and the
lintel of the houses where they eat it... V 13.
"the blood shall be a sign for YOU on the
houses where you are. And when I SEE the
blood, I shall pass over, and let the plague not
come on you to destroy you when I strike the
land of Mitsrayim (Egypt)." (Shemoth/Exodus
12:5; 7; 13)

Life is in the blood. *"For the life of the flesh is in the*
blood, and I have given it to you upon the altar to make
atonement for your lives, for it is the blood that makes
atonement for the life." (Wayyiqra/Leviticus 17:11)

YHVH's covenant promise to send a Savior and its fulfillment is in the person of Yeshua Ha Mashiach (Jesus Christ).

"And Elohim said to the serpent, "Because
you have done this, you are cursed more than
all livestock and more than every beast of the
field. On your belly you are to go, and eat dust
all the days of your life. V 15, And I put enmity
between you and the woman, and between

*seed and her Seed. (First promise of the
ssiah) He shall crush your head, and you
all crush His heel."* (Bereshith/Genesis
:14) Also read Yeshayahu/Isaiah chapter 53.

Being born again means that you have recognized,
acknowledged, accepted, believed, and confessed with your
mouth that Yeshua Ha Mashiach is the Son of YHVH, the
perfect sacrificial Lamb, who took all our sin and paid the
price for redemption, when He died, was buried and rose
again from the dead. He shed His own blood for you and for
me. Yeshua is the fulfillment of YHVH's covenant promise
and provision of a Redeeming Savior. It is only through
Yeshua that we enter into the Holy of Holies and into the
presence of YHVH. All we have to do is humble ourselves,
repent of our sin, profess the Name of Yeshua, and begin
our lifetime commitment with YHVH our Father, Yeshua
Ha Mashiach – His Son, and Ruach Ha Kodesh – His Holy
Spirit.

> *"If I shut up the heavens and there is no rain,
> or if I command the locusts to devour the
> land, or if I send pestilence among MY
> people, and My people upon whom MY
> NAME is called, shall HUMBLE themselves
> and pray and seek MY FACE, and TURN
> FROM their EVIL WAYS, THEN I shall
> HEAR from the heavens, and FORGIVE
> their sin and heal their land."* (2 Dibre
> haYamim/ 2 Chronicles 7:13-14)

To "turn from" means to repent of our hardness of heart,
our disobedience, rebellious actions, or anything that keeps
us separated from YHVH our Father. When we do that…
WE ARE BORN AGAIN!!!!

Will you cry out with a repentant heart? Will you say, "Yes YHVH... Yes. I want to know Your Son. I want to walk in the covenant that His blood made available to me. I receive Yeshua Ha Mashiach as my Adonai/Lord, and my Savior. I want to walk in the power, comfort, teaching, and guidance of Your Ruach Ha Kodesh (Holy Spirit)." Whether you are Jew or Gentile, God desires for you to be complete through His Son, Yeshua.

If you have just made this confession, then you are born again, and have the Ruach Ha Kodesh (or Holy Spirit) living inside of you. You have become a child of YHVH! You will find that your life and your priorities will begin to change. You will have a hunger for reading His Word, and His Kingdom will begin to increase in your life, day-by-day. The road you have now stepped onto is one of faith. It is a Narrow Gate we walk through, and a narrow path we trod.

> *"Enter in through the narrow gate! Because the gate is wide-and the way is broad-that leads to destruction, and there are many who enter in through it. Because the gate is narrow and the way is hard pressed which leads to life, and there are few who find it."*
> (Matthew 7:13-14)

There are times when you will know His presence with such certainty, and times when you will feel alone. But know this:

> *"You are of Elohim, little children, and have overcome them, because HE who is IN YOU is GREATER than he who is in the world."*
> (1 John 4:4)

Welcome to your new life and your new family! We are

each grafted into the whole house of Yisrael through our Jewish Savior, Yeshua Ha Mashiach. This is a lifetime commitment on earth, and our promise of eternal life in glory with our Savior!

Special End Note for Seasoned Intercessors

✦

For those intercessors that have an interest in spiritual mapping, I found an interesting connection between this teaching I have covered on the Gates, and spiritual mapping. I first made the discovery when I was driving through my hometown, Jacksonville, Florida. While driving around I-295, I realized that in the different parts of the perimeter of the city the way I was praying in tongues would change. In fact, I was on my way to a Pastor's home, I missed the exit and found myself driving from the west side of the city to the east side. I felt the spiritual climate change so significantly that I asked the Lord, "What was that?" Especially when I was driving through the west side of the city, I could feel that I was under oppression and heaviness. As the Spirit of the Lord began to show me what was happening in those areas, He led me to Ezekiel 48.

> *"And these are the exits of the city: on the north side, 4,500 cubits by measurement, shall be the gates of the city, named for the*

> *tribes of Israel, three gates toward the north: the gate of Reuben, one; the gate of Judah, one; the gate of Levi, one. And on the east side, 4,500 cubits, shall be three gates: the gate of Joseph, one; the gate of Benjamin, one; the gate of Dan, one. And on the south side, 4,500 cubits by measurement, shall be three gates: the gate of Simeon, one; the gate of Issachar, one; the gate of Zebulun, one. On the west side, 4,500 cubits, shall be three gates: the gate of Gad, one; the gate of Asher, one; the gate of Naphtali, one. "The city shall be 18,000 cubits round about; and the name of the city from that day shall be, 'The LORD is there.'"* (Ezekiel 48:30-35)

Using this pattern from Ezekiel, I began to take a look at the spiritual climate of my city, Jacksonville, Florida. Keep in mind, the material we covered regarding the attacking strongholds (you may need to refer back to that section which is in chapter 10), to get the clearest picture of the information given to us here in the book of Ezekiel.

The North Gates are: Reuben, Judah and Levi
The Strongholds that attack from the North are: Anti-Messiah Spirit, Spirit of Perversion, and Lying Spirit

The East Gates are: Joseph, Benjamin, and Dan
The Strongholds that attack from the East are: Spirit of Infirmity, Spirit of Pride, and Spirit of Bondage

The South Gates are: Simeon, Issachar, and Zebulon
The Strongholds that attack from the South are: Deaf & Dumb Spirit, Spirit of Whoredom, Familiar Spirits

The West Gates are: Gad, Asher, and Naphtali
The Strongholds that attack from the West are: Spirit of
Fear, Spirit of Heaviness, and Spirit of Jealousy

When I placed this pattern over my own home city, I
found that the manifestations of these strongholds did often
appear in the neighborhoods and sections of the city that
geographically coordinated with the information revealed in
Ezekiel chapter 48.

In March of 2003, I was in Israel and was asked to share
the Gates teaching with the staff of Emmaus Way Ministries
in Tel Aviv. I just gave them a quick overview of the teaching and the staff members wanted to know where the
strongholds were located in the city, what the redemptive
keys were, as well as the location of the gates. As I began to
relate this information to them they took out a map of the
city of Tel Aviv and they were amazed at how the manifestations of the strongholds were predominant in the locations
of the city corresponding with the text from Ezekiel 48. This
is not to say that the manifestations only occur in those locations, but it became apparent that there was a more prevalent
matching of areas and strongholds that could not be coinci-
dental. This information afforded them the foreknowledge
to send teams of intercessors to the areas to specifically
target those strongholds. Glory to God.

If you apply this same strategy to your city or area of the
country, you may also find some "clues" as to how to pray
effectively through the gates for your region. I would love
to hear from those of you who further investigate this intercession key. Please feel free to contact the ministry office
using the contact information that appears at the back of the
book to tell me about your discoveries.

For information regarding speaking engagements, acquiring additional copies of the books and or tapes, you may contact us through e-mail.

E-mail us at ipni@aol.com

When ordering tapes or CD's we suggest the following donations to the Gates of Prayer Ministries. If you have an interest in purchasing more copies of *Weapons of Mass Deliverance*, please visit the publisher online at www.xulonpress.com. Click on "online bookstore."

Gates of Prayer 5 tape album $25
Guarding Your Conversation Cassette $5
Guarding Your Conversation Compact Disc $7
4 Cornerstones of Ministry Cassette $5
4 Cornerstones of Ministry Compact Disc $7

Please add shipping and handling $5.95 to the order.

If you have an interest in purchasing the fasting book that I recommended in chapter 5, entitled, *A Walk in the Wilderness – The Spiritual Discipline of Fasting*, by Lori Greenwood, please visit the publisher online at www.xulonpress.com. Click on "online bookstore." For a complete list of books and tapes by Dr. Lori Greenwood, visit www.thevisionlink.com, or write to Lori Greenwood Ministries, Inc, PO Box 446, Broomall, PA 19008-0446. LGMinistries@cs.com

CPSIA information can be obtained
at www.ICGtesting.com
Printed in the USA
BVHW030221220520
580125BV00001B/141